W9-AWJ-609

POLAND

THROUGHOUT THE CENTURIES TOWARDS THE NEW MILLENNIUM

Dear Jon:

Having in mind your interest in traveling to Poland one day, this album should give you a fair preview of what to expect to see after crossing the Polish border.

most respectfully

[illegible signature]

Warner Korwacki

your August 2003 intern

From where my Homeland is...
to André Jr. and Tina, my children born in the land of Washington
with all my love

Their Father
Andrzej Frukacz

POLAND

THROUGHOUT THE CENTURIES TOWARDS THE NEW MILLENNIUM

Photographs

Paweł Jaroszewski

Texts

Krzysztof Burek
Paweł Huelle
Rev. Professor Józef Tischner
Jerzy Waldorff
Professor Jacek Woźniakowski

Wydawnictwo Andrzej Frukacz

Exlibris

Galeria Polskiej Książki

POLAND

The Birth of the State

Krzysztof Burek

POLAND

Historians have no doubt that the core of the Piast state, whose earliest recorded history dates back to the second half of the 10th century, was territory belonging to the Polanie tribe. It was situated in the central part of Wielkopolska. It was there that essential social and political changes were initiated and important decisions of great consequence were made. It was also there that Poland was born.

Ostrów Lednicki, the largest of the four islands on Lake Lednica, bore witness to the first hours of our national history. A large stronghold was built on this site. It was used as the seat of the ruler and after adopting the Christian faith it also played the role of a religious center.

After sailing through the lake and reaching the shore of this unique island, one cannot resist being overcome by emotions at the sight of the remains of the centuries-old architecture. The chapel and the palladium evoke the images of the times of Mieszko. For over one hundred and fifty years these structures have been objects of interest of archaeologists and architecture historians. A dozen years or so ago, archaeologists discovered two characteristic hollows in the ancient floor of the chapel, dating from before 966. They are baptisteries connected with the small adjoining building considered to have been a bishop's residence (*episcopium*).

It can be assumed that here, on the Island of Ostrów Lednicki, on Holy Saturday in 966, the baptism ceremony of Prince Mieszko I and his court took place.

We stand silent facing the substantial evidence of that breakthrough event in the history of Poland, when the water of baptism was sprinkled on our native land for the first time. That is where the Christian era in the history of the Polish people began more than one thousand years ago. The heir of that history, the generation of the Third Republic of Poland, erected a metal structure over those holy relics. This is the Gate to the Third Millennium. It is shaped like a fish – a symbol of Jesus Christ. In June 1997, a helicopter carrying Pope John Paul II flew over it. The young people gathered on Ostrów Lednicki listened eagerly to the words of the Pope. He encouraged them to preserve the heritage of their ancestors and to make their lives in the Third Millennium based on the tenets of religion, hope and love. The young people answered that appeal by repeating the baptismal oath. Those were the same words uttered on that site by the first historic ruler of Poland, "in the name of the Father, and the Son and the Holy Ghost."

Setting out from Ostrów Lednicki, a place which enjoys the status of a national symbol, we begin our wandering to many other places in our homeland, such as Gniezno and Poznań, where reminders of our historical and cultural identity have been preserved. These relics of the past are part of our heritage, which we contribute to the mainstream of the restored unity of Christian Europe.

At the end of the 9th century, a small stronghold was established at Ostrów Lednicki. An oval earthen rampart is among its only remains. Some fragments of the foundations of the church that was situated at the foot of the stronghold and two tombs also survived there. King Boleslaus the Brave's son – Otton or Bezprym – might have been buried in one of them. The remains of the chapel and of the Prince's palace are among the most precious traces of the early history of the Polish state. The church functioned as a baptistery – a place where baptismal rites were performed. The baptismal pools uncovered in the years 1988–1989, testify to that.

Gnezdun Civitas – such a name appeared on a denarius coin from c. 992. In its corrupted version – *Civitas Schinegsche* – it appears in the document called *Dagome iudex*, which was drawn up sometime between 990 and 992. It says that Mieszko I and his wife, Oda, make their realm subject to St. Peter, or in other words to the Apostolic See.

Gnezdun Civitas is the name testifying to the historical transformations that took place in the 10th century in Wielkopolska. They involved the establishment of the Gniezno state – a political, economic, military and cultural center of the Polanie tribe – as well as the establishment of its spatial structure whose dominant centers were the settlements of Gniezno, Poznań, Giecz and Ostrów Lednicki.

As legend has it, on top of Lech's Mountain, where the metropolitan cathedral basilica dedicated to the Assumption of the Holy Virgin Mary seems to touch the clouds with its soaring towers, a white eagle – the centuries-old symbol of Poland – made its nest. In reality, the hill became the "nest" of the Polanie tribe – the creators of the Polish state.

The archaeological research conducted inside the cathedral revealed some remainders of a fire-place, which had been used for a long time and which had been attended to carefully. In all likelihood, it was a place of the pagan cult and it is assumed that Gniezno was its main center.

The first Christian rulers of Gniezno – the cradle of the Piast dynasty – made their capital also a religious and ecclesiastical center. On this spot, in the first church built on Lech's Mountain and founded by Mieszko I, the mortal remains of Adalbert Strawnikowicz were entombed. He was the bishop of Prague, a friend of Otto III and an apostle of Jesus Christ, who died the death of a martyr in the area of the lower Vistula River, where he had been sent by Boleslaus the Brave.

In the year 1000, in the presence of Emperor Otto III and Prince Boleslaus the Brave, at the tomb of the Martyr, who was made Saint in 999, papal legates solemnly announced the decision of the Pope, Silvester II, who established an independent ecclesiastical province in Poland. It was the Metropolis of Gniezno, which consisted of the Archdiocese of Gniezno and the newly created bishoprics in Kołobrzeg, Kraków and Wrocław. The political meeting, known as the Convention of Gniezno, which took place in connection with Emperor Otto's pilgrimage to St. Adalbert's tomb, focused on the idea of creating a universal European empire. Poland was to be its rightful member.

The first cathedral in Gniezno was plundered and destroyed in 1038 during the invasion of the Bohemian Prince Brzetysław. Among its ruins, wild animals made their lairs and burrows, but it was soon rebuilt and consecrated in the years 1069 and 1097. The most magnificent reminder of the first cathedral are the famous Doors of Gniezno.

The construction of the Gothic cathedral was initiated in the 14th century by Archbishop Jarosław Bogoria of Skotniki. His work was continued by his successors, Archbishop Janusz Suchywilk and Archbishop Bodzanta. In January 1945, the church caught fire as a result of gunfire. It destroyed the richly decorated interior that had been given its final character in the Baroque times. During the post-war reconstruction the cathedral was given its former Gothic style.

The cathedral in Gniezno is a place of worship and the shrine of St. Adalbert, a patron of Poland (in the 12th century St. Stanislaus became the second patron). It played an essential role in the integration of the Polish national and ecclesiastical life, especially before 1772. Until the year 1300 the coronation ceremonies of the Polish kings were held there. Since the 14th century, the Archbishop of Gniezno has held the position of the Primate of Poland – a special guardian of the religious and national unity. He also used to hold the function of an interrex (temporary king) when the country had no king.
In the recent Polish history two Archbishops of Gniezno made names for themselves. They were Cardinals August Hlond and Stefan Wyszyński – the people who are symbols of the struggle for the rights of the Church and of the Nation in post-war Poland subjugated by the communist system.

The shrine and mausoleum of St. Adalbert, was founded in the 17th century. A relief image of the figure of the Saint is presented on the cover of his restored silver coffin (destroyed in 1986.) "The blood which St. Adalbert shed bears forever new spiritual fruit. All of Poland benefited from it in the earliest days of its statehood and in the successive centuries. The Convention of Gniezno opened for Poland the way to unity with the entire family of the European countries. At the threshold of the second millenium the Polish nation was given the right to participate in the process of creating a new Europe hand in hand with other nations. Thus, St. Adalbert is a great patron of our continent, which was then getting unit-

ed in the name of Christ. The life, as well as the death of the Saint Martyr, constitutes the basis of the European identity and unity."

The Doors of Gniezno are a pair of doors from the Romanesque cathedral, cast in bronze in the last quarter of the 12th century, during the reign of Prince Mieszko III the Old. It is believed that its founder was the Archbishop of Gniezno – Jan of Brzezie – or his successor, Archbishop Zdzisław.

On the exterior side of the two doors are 18 fields with bas-relief figural scenes, depicting the events from the life of St. Adalbert – his martyrdom, the act of buying back his body by Prince Boleslaus the Brave and the placement of his remains in the church dedicated to the Assumption of the Holy Virgin Mary in Gniezno. The impressive fringe with figural, animal and plant motifs accompanies the vivid narrative whose protagonist is St. Adalbert – the patron of the country. The Doors of Gniezno – an exquisite artifact of the Romanesque culture – are rich in symbolic and theological meaning. They are also a document recording the realia of that epoch – the appearance of weapons and objects, the portraits of dukes, knights, clergymen and the pagan Prussians.

The art of the masters who made the door can be admired inside the church. The eye is caught by the ornamentation of the bars in the side chapels.

The aisles of the cathedral are 18 meters high and they are covered by Gothic ribbed vaults. The aisles are ringed with fourteen chapels built at the turn of the 14th century and then remodeled according to the principles of the Baroque style. The portals of the chapels are closed with ornamental bars, which are real masterpieces of smithsmanship. The history and development of this craft – beginning in Gothic times, through the Renaissance up to Baroque – is inscribed in those elaborate ornaments.

This is a monument of Boleslaus the Brave, the first ruler of Poland to wear the royal crown (in 1025.) The memory of his deeds has survived for centuries. He annexed a large part of Pomerania, the regions of Kraków and Sandomierz, Silesia, Grody Czerwieńskie, Lusatia and, for a limited period of time, Slovakia, to the lands of the Piast Dynasty. Boleslaus the Brave was a victorious commander in the battles against Germany and Ruthenia. It was he who chipped his own sword upon striking the gate of Kiev. The weapon then became the coronation sword of the Polish kings and it was called "Szczerbiec" (meaning "chipped".)

Who does not know the legendary story about Prince Popiel, the ruler of Gniezno, who was driven away from his realm with his offspring and then eaten up by mice? The historical background of that gloomy legend involved probably some authentic event – a violent overthrow of the local prince. According to *Kronika wielkopolska*, written in the 12th century, the place traditionally associated with Prince Popiel was situated in Kruszwica, near Lake Gopło. (The so-called Mouse Tower, which can be seen there, is the only remainder of the castle built during the reign of King Casimir the Great). Gall the Anonymous, the author of the 12th-century *Polish Chronicle*, wrote that: "Kruszwica has plenty of wealth and many knights."

Kruszwica was a favorite town of Mieszko III, the second king of Poland (1025–1034), who would frequently stay there with his court. It was from there the warriors of Boleslaus the Wrymouth set off on their conquest of Pomerania. In connection with the planned Christianization of Pomerania a bishopric was established in Kruszwica in the first half of the 12th century (soon it was moved to Włocławek). The Romanesque walls of the monumental collegiate erected from 1120 to 1140 by the Benedictine monks, who came from the region of the Flemish-German border, testify to the former grandeur of Kruszwica, which was once the center of the economic and political life of Kujawy.

The Birth of the State

Krzysztof Burek

The edifice of the town hall in Poznań is an icon of the municipal council that has governed the city for centuries. The City of Poznań, founded in 1253, on the left bank of the Warta River, in the center of the Wielkopolska-Kujawy Lowland, on a junction of a few international communication trails, quickly developed into the cultural and administrative center of Wielkopolska. As early as the 13th century, during the reign of Prince Przemysław I, the capital of the province was moved from Gniezno to Poznań for good.

At the turn of the 13th century, the town hall was built in the middle of the Market Square. Many times remodeled and embellished, it has survived in the Renaissance form which it was given in the years 1550–1560. The slender tower is a later addition going back to the 18th century.

In the times of the First Republic, Poznań belonged to the largest cities in Poland, surpassed only by Kraków and Lviv. There were numerous workshops of clothiers, tanners and furriers. The city was one of the most important centers on the commercial trails leading from Lithuania to Ruthenia and Germany and from Kraków to Szczecin.

It is inscribed into the history of Polish culture and science. In the 13th century Poznań became an important historiographic center in Wielkopolska. Among others, *The Wielkopolska Chronicle* was written there. Famous are also such institutions as the Lubrański Academy founded in 1519 and the Raczyński Library (1829).

The role Poznań played during the partitions is well remembered. It was then a prominent center of culture, of scientific and political thought, as well as of the diverse social actions resisting the process of Germanization.

It is the capital of the region which was involved in the successful Wielkopolska Uprising of 1918. In the times of the Second Republic the International Poznań Fair (continued also after the war) and the Universal National Exposition were held there.

In the post-war history of Poland, Poznań also has a special status. In June 1956, it was the scene of the first mass protests of workers, whose motto "bread and liberty" stood for the values which were then quite scarce. With much bloodshed the protests were mercilessly suppressed.

WYSTAWA
ROBOCZA

The Market Square in Poznań was rebuilt according to the Baroque and neoclassical styles after its destruction during World War II. The tower of the town hall, built in 1550 by master Giovanni Battista Quadro, dominates over the roofs of the houses in the Market.

Ostrów Tumski is a significant place in the history of Poznań and Poland. A small stronghold was established here already in the first half of the 10th century, possibly near the ford on the Warta River.

The first, pre-Romanesque cathedral was erected here in the year 968. After it had been destroyed, the construction of the church was continued in the subsequent centuries, despite the various occurring catastrophes and fires.

The Archcathedral Basilica dedicated to the Apostles Saint Peter and Saint Paul, was reconstructed after the end of the last war. It was then given its former Gothic shape.

On the left of the Cathedral is a red, brick late-Gothic church, dating from the years 1431–1444, dedicated to the Holy Virgin Mary. As tradition has it, it stands on the site of the first church that existed within the stronghold.

The cathedral is topped with a brace of towers – two main ones at 62 meters tall; the three minor ones serve as turrets-lanterns. Throughout the centuries the church witnessed some significant events in the history of Poland, such as royal nuptials and coronations, as well as the inauguration celebrations of the Millenium of Christianity in Poland in 1966. The cathedral is also a royal necropolis. The first rulers of Poland – Mieszko I and Boleslaus the Brave are buried here. The famous Golden Chapel is dedicated to them. Below, in the crypt, stand some of the remains of the walls of the first cathedral as well as the fragments of the baptismal font.

The parish church, whose construction was started in the mid-17th century, is a splendid example of the Baroque style. Its interior is richly decorated with stucco-work and paintings. The low aisles are full of columns and sculptures.

At dusk, the Renaissance attic of the town hall presents itself against the background of the evening sky. Nearby, one can see a Rococo fountain of Prozerpina, dating from 1766, and a bit further on the neoclassical façade of the Działyński Palace embellished with columns.

The National Sanctuary

Krzysztof Burek

In Częstochowa, a town situated on the historical border between the Małopolska and Silesia regions, there is a hill called Jasna Góra, which is one of the country's most important religious sites – the spiritual capital of Poland.

In the 14th century, located on the site over which impressive Basilica of Jasna Góra towers today, was a wooden Church of the Holy Virgin Mary, the Birth-giver. In 1382, the ruler of this region, Duke Ladislaus of Opole, transferred control of Częstochowa Church to the Brothers of St. Paul, the First Hermit, also known as the Pauline monks, who came to Poland from Hungary. Two years later, in 1384, the brothers received an unusual gift from the Duke, an icon, featuring a dark-faced Madonna with child, which he had brought here from Bełz.

As the years passed, Jasna Góra became the most famous place of worship devoted to the Virgin Mary in Poland. The iraculous Icon of Our Lady draws innumerable crowds. On her face there are two scars, mementoes of a Hussite assault in the 15th century. Every August, large numbers of pilgrims visit the sanctuary. After many days of pilgrimage the moment finally arrives. The slender tower of the Basilica looming on the horizon, announces the end of the journey and the pilgrims' approaching encounter in Chapel of the Miraculous Icon with the Mother of Jesus, advocate of graces, consoler of the sorrowful, our intermediary in the dialogue with God.

Poles still remember the defiant defence of the church on Jasna Góra during the Swedish invasion in 1655. A hundred years later, in 1770, the Bar Confederates under the command of Kazimierz Pułaski, who later became a hero in the struggle of the United States to secure its independence, successfully defended the sanctuary from the Russian army.

Jasna Góra is the nation's shrine and bastion of faith and hope, especially during difficult times. ("When all the lights over Poland went out, there has always been the Saint of Częstochowa" – interestingly, these are the words of Hans Frank, the Nazi General Governor during World War II.)

On Church holidays devoted to the Holy Virgin and on national holidays, thousands of worshipers gather on a vast square lying at the foot of the monastery. The first Vows of the Nation were taken on this square in 1954, a program of religious, moral and national rebirth devised by Cardinal Stefan Wyszyński, the Primate of the Millennium, who was imprisoned at that time.

On May 3, 1966, on the holiday of Maria the Queen of the Polish Crown and the thousand anniversary of the baptism of Poland by Duke Mieszko, a solemn *Te Deum Laudamus* was sung here. An empty armchair for Pope Paul VI, who was refused entry to Poland by the communist government, was placed next to the Icon of the Holy Virgin. In June 1979, John Paul II kneeled before the Jasna Góra shrine during his first pilgrimage to his home country, as he wanted "to hear the heart of the Church and the heart of the Fatherland beat in the heart of the Mother."

Jasna Góra was gradually transformed into the "Fortalium Marianum" fortress. Fine examples of 17th- and 18th-century military architecture and engineering art have survived to the present day – a rectangle of earthen fortifications surrounded by a wall, side bastions and a wide moat.
Crowds of pilgrims walk over the top of the ramparts, stopping at the stations of Via Crucis and the monument of Prior August Kordecki, heroic defender of the monastery during the Swedish invasion in the 17th century.

Since 1650, the Icon of Our Lady has been kept in a separate chapel, one of the finest works of Polish Baroque art. The oak altar, covered with an ebony facing and silver ornaments, was founded by Jerzy Osoliński, the Great Chancellor of the Crown. An ornamented grate donated by Primate Maciej Łubieński, separates the altar from the chapel interior. Legend has it that the Holy Icon of Jasna Góra was painted by St. Lucas himself. It is believed to have been painted on the board from a table at which the Holy Family used to sit in Nazareth.

Incessant prayer, full of trust and devotion, continues at the chapel of the Miraculous Icon, the Queen of the Polish Crown:

"Mother who knows us, be with thy children,
Mother who knows us, lead us to your Son."

The interior of the basilica church dedicated to the Assumption of the Holy Virgin Mary and to the Discovery of the Holy Cross is adorned with stucco-works and with murals by K. Dankwart.
A vast square at the foothills of the Jasna Góra monastery is a meeting place of pilgrims. At night many candles are lit near the lonely figure of Our Lady.

The Vistula River, often called the Queen of the Polish rivers, has its sources somewhere on the slopes of the Silesian Beskid Mountains, among the spruces of the Mt Barania Góra Nature Reserve. The thickets of one of the most precious spruce forests in Europe, known as the so-called Istebna species, hide the sources of the Czarna Wisełka and the Biała Wisełka, which join their waters with the brooks of Roztoczny and Wątrobny. In the town of Wisła both the Czarna Wisełka and the Biała Wisełka form one river – the Little Vistula – whose waters flow on getting mightier and mightier. For a number of centuries, the Vistula River Valley constituted a commercial trail that ran from the Carpathian foothills

to the Baltic Sea, connecting small villages as well as the renowned cities situated near the river.

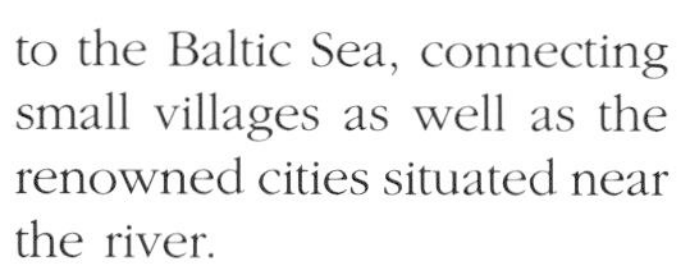

The monasteries whose white edifices prominent on the hills towering over the Vistula River Valley are unique places that resist the passage of time. Not far from Kraków, stand two old abbeys – of the Cameldolite monks in Bielany and of the Benedictine order in Tyniec.

The monastery of the Cameldolites in Bielany in Kraków came into being on this site owing to the efforts of the Great Crown Marshal, Mikołaj Wolski, whose family crest was Półkozic. For almost four hundred years (since 1604) the spiritual sons of St. Romualdus (who died in 1027) have lived here as hermits, following the Benedictine principle – "Ora et labora" (Pray and work.)

According to experts, the mighty architectural complex, including the immense church, belongs to the most beautiful pearls of the late Baroque style not only in Kraków, but elsewhere. Two significant architectural concepts, imposed by the sequestered life, visibly distinguish the Cameldolites from the Benedictines of Tyniec, whose ancient abbey is situated on the opposite side of the Vistula River. The first difference consists of the existence of the little hermit huts, known by the Greek name of *erems* (hermitages). The hermits live in them completely alone. They are people endowed with a special gift – the love of God manifesting itself in their secluded life.

The other difference is the so-called monastery wall, which surrounds the one-hectare area of the monastery on "Silver Mountain." This special kind of separation, known as the papal enclosure, makes it impossible for women to enter the hermitage and for the monks to leave it without permission. The atmosphere created in this way is suitable for conducting a fruitful sequestered life within the monastic family.

The Benedictine Abbey towers on a steep limestone rock, 40 meters above the Vistula. It was probably founded by Casimir the Restorer in the year 1044. The towers of the Baroque church of St. Paul and St. Peter, dating back to the years 1618–22, are located on the site of two former churches – one Romanesque and the other Gothic. The place is quite unusual – as if it were a watch-tower overlooking the Vistula's meander. In the summer, the organ concerts that are held here attract crowds of music-lovers.

In fact, any activity going on behind the monastery wall is organized in such a way that whatever the hermits do, should be done for the glory of God. The entire plan of the day, dictated by the famous Benedictine principle – "Pray and work" – and sanctioned by centuries of tradition, constitutes a special form of the Cameldolite asceticism. The monks compare it to the proverbial soil which should be cultivated in order to bear spiritual fruit. Sometimes the atmosphere of seclusion makes the ordained ones wait very long for that fruit.

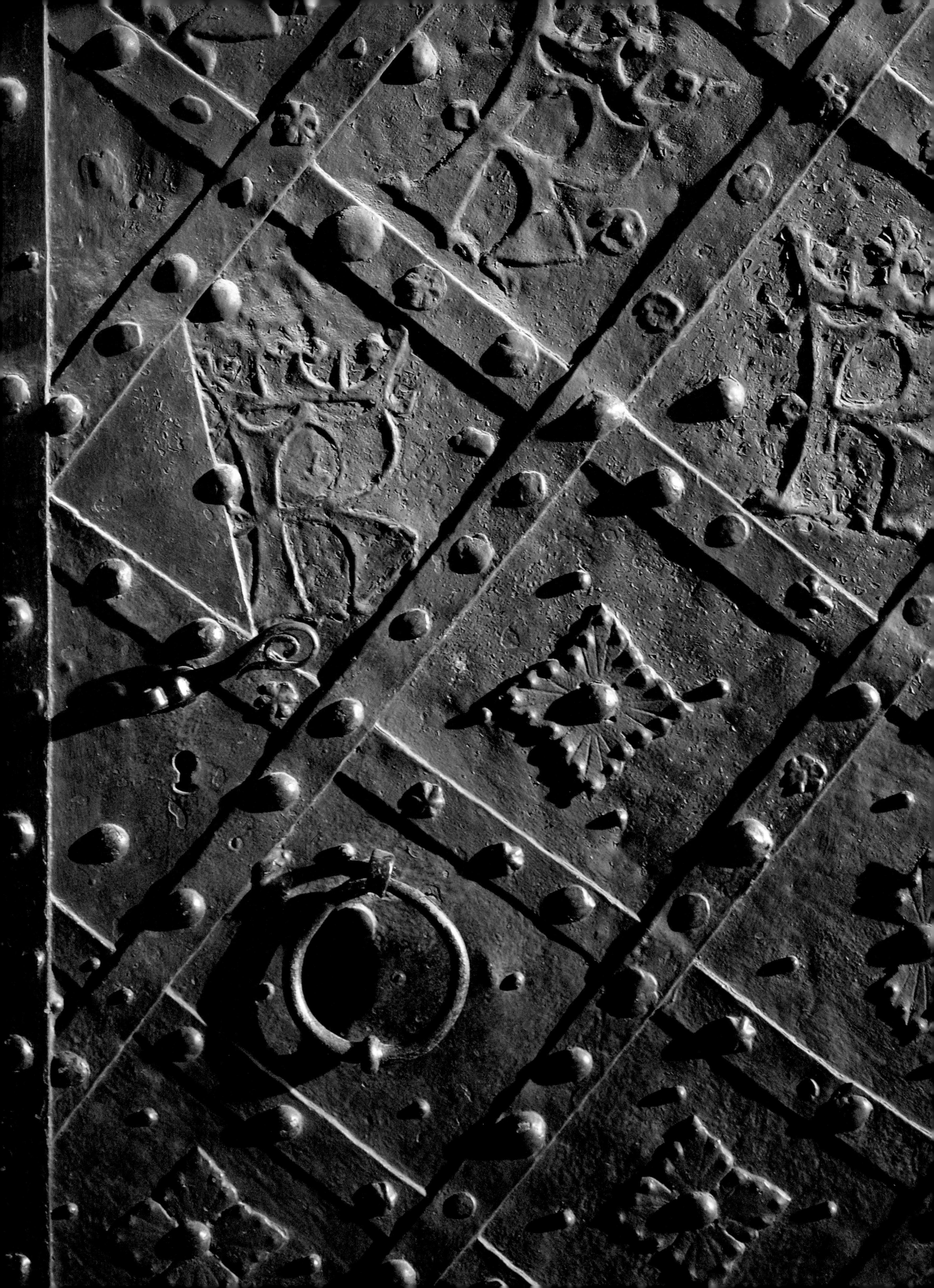

Kraków – An Open City

Professor Jacek Woźniakowski

Like other historical cities that miraculously escaped destruction over time, Kraków boasts several centers where its vital functions are focused, clearly showing the city's symbolic meaning. Consider its Main Square and the University.

Since the mid-13th century when the boldly planned city received its charter, the Main Square has been at the crossing of important trade routes – north-south and east-west. The historians of Hansa maintain that Wrocław and Kraków were the most distant outposts of this North-European union of commercial cities.

They identify major goods that passed through the city in different times: from the west – salt, wine, cloth and wool; from the east and from the local region – timber, grass and leather; from the north – fish and amber.

Later on there were weapons, textiles and costumes, varied furniture, prints and etchings which arrived from the south, the Near East and from the Netherlands.... Imagine the Main Square, bustling with life, full of colorful, multilingual crowds from all over the world along with the dignified representatives of Kraków's merchants, curious about or perhaps already acquainted with the world, and spectators of all kinds. It is one of the symbols of the role Krakow has played over the centuries.

Another symbol of this international development is the oldest building of the Kraków Academy, a hundred years younger than the Main Square, and known eventually as the Jagiellonian University. The building is the Collegium Maius, with its charming Gothic courtyard. In one of its rooms we can see astronomical instruments believed to be used by Copernicus during his studies there, and, indeed, dating from even before his times.

Next to them we can find the first globe on which a small part of east coast of America was shown less than twenty years after it had been chartered. Finally, next to the globe we can see a photograph of the surface of the moon autographed by Neil Armstrong, the first man ever to set foot on the Moon.

In the era of Internet, the conquest of the Moon may seem an old story to the thousands of Kraków's students. Young people form a considerable part of Kraków's population of less than a million, along with a number of outstanding personages of the older generation – researchers, writers, painters, musicians and people from the theater. Numerous young people will become witnesses and co-creators of unexpected twists of history which seems to travel faster and faster... including the history of the city itself, over which Wawel Hill and the well-lit cupolas of many church towers can be seen.

Among these, the colorful towers of St. Mary's Basilica with the light sifting through its ancient stained-glass windows onto old wooden polyptychs inside, along with the stone crucifix by Wit Stwosz (Veit Stoss.) Trade still flourishes in the stalls of the 16th-century Cloth Hall in the middle of the Main Square. Just outside, under Kraków's misty sky, vendors sell their flowers as they have done *ab urbe condita* – since the establishment of the city.

When focusing on the intertwining of Kraków's different eras and cultures, with a bleeding heart we go to the Kazimierz district. Once bustling with life, then dying after the barbaric Nazi demolition, we now see its synagogues being restored, its colorful Gothic churches emerging from the surrounding greenery and the legendary Skałka Church in which the baroque and Rococo styles spring from Gothic foundations.

On a stroll from the Main Square towards Wawel one shouldn't miss the Gothic Franciscan Church with its breath-taking art nouveau stained-glass windows by Stanisław Wyspiański.

Stop for a while a little further on at St. Mary Magdalene's Square at the middle of Kanonicza Street, across from the magnificent Church of SS. Peter and Paul, modeled from the Jesuit Gesu, adjacent to the Romanesque St. Andrew's Church with its white defensive towers that once guarded the passage from the city center to the center of royal power headquartered on Wawel Hill.

While facing these two churches, on the left is a Gothic house in brick, while on the right is the Renaissance Collegium Iuridicum with a charming miniature courtyard. Behind us is a Neo-classical house in a line of medieval and Renaissance dwellings of cathedral canons with discreetly hidden passages and rear gardens. The Rev. Karol Wojtyła (Pope John Paul II) lived for more than ten years in one of these dwellings in very modest conditions.

And finally, further on is Wawel Hill, with its famous Italian-style courtyard, with columns believed to have been painted red with golden capitals. Next to the castle is the older cathedral where two saints, Stanislaus of Szczepanów and Queen Jadwiga, found their final rest, as did other kings, national heroes and poets, and where all eras of our history superimpose in a natural way.

A steep set of steps ascends from the western entrance that is guarded by two towers that are completely different from one another. Perhaps this design was an attempt to suppress the effect of the symmetry of the vast southern facade of the cathedral with its two chapels on both sides of the entrance. Yet, this symmetry is already softened with the verdigris copper roof of one chapel, and the gold-plated roof of the other. One was built by the kings of the Jagiellon dynasty who came here from Lithuania, while the other was built by the Vasas from Scandinavia; the cathedral is primarily of the Piast era.

Looking from Wawel across the river we can see the contemporary lines of the Japanese Art Center, flowing like the Vistula River itself. What better symbols of the openness of Kraków can we find?

The ornamented facades of old tenement houses, numerous nooks and crannies, church towers and the Renaissance ornaments of the Cloth Hall contribute to the charming and unique character of the Market Square in Kraków, which is one of the largest city squares in Europe. It is surrounded with a regular network of streets. Only one of them, leading to Wawel Hill is oblique. The southern corner of the Square is dominated by the sky-reaching towers of St. Mary's Church while the opposite corner by the Gothic Town Hall Tower. Near the outlet of Ulica Grodzka the Market is closed with a small edifice of St. Adalbert's – a Romanesque church, which for centuries has been standing on this spot – once a junction of commercial trails. →

The Market Square in Kraków has for centuries been the site of important events in the life of the City and of the Polish state. The history of the Cloth Hall began in the 13th century, when King Boleslaus the Chaste, in the charter of Kraków, dated 1257, promised to build the vending stalls in the city. Not long afterwards, in 1306, Ladislas the Short granted the privilege of storage to the city. Henceon, the traveling merchants were obliged to stop in Kraków and to sell their goods through the local vendors.

In the years 1380–1400 the vending stalls were enlarged and in that way the Cloth Hall came into being. After a fire in 1555 it was rebuilt according to the Renaissance style by Giovanni Maria Padovano. The building was given its final shape by Tomasz Pryliński, an architect who was in charge of its restoration at the end of the 19th century.

Like in the past, all day long, the Cloth Hall is alive with activity and the vending stalls are visited both by Cracovians and tourists. When dusk falls and with the onset of silence, the filigree arcades and the dainty elements of the Renaissance attic bathe in darkness; it almost seems that the old walls start spinning stories of the merchants of old...

The tops of the Wawel Cathedral towers, covered with greenish patina, and the dome of the Sigismund Chapel glittering with gold are the most characteristic element in the panorama of Kraków.

The slim, Gothic form of St. Mary's Church seems to be a guardian of peace in the Royal City. Since the 14th century the taller of the two towers functioned as the city watchtower. Atop it the trumpeters kept their watch over the city. The lower tower – with its five bells (including the so-called "Half-Sigismund" which is the largest of them) – was the belfry. In its present shape of a three-aisled basilica with a transept the church has existed since the beginning of the 14th century. It was erected at that time on the site of the former Romanesque church destroyed by the Tartars around 1241.

The present luster of the interior of St. Mary's Basilica is a result of the comprehensive restoration works carried out during the last ten years.
The colorful murals are the work of Jan Matejko. Together with his two students, Stanisław Wyspiański and Józef Mehoffer, he created the new, 19th-century interior decorations. At the same time Tadeusz Stryjeński, an architect, restored the former Gothic character to the church. However, he managed to preserve the works of art which accumulated there throughout the previous centuries.
The arches of the side chapels make the space of the church dynamic and they direct one's attention to the chancel, where a crucifix is suspended in the rood-screen, under the blue vault, adorned with golden stars. The light assumes the colors of the stained-glass windows, closing the 14th-century chancel.
The focal point of the church is an altar created by master Veit Stoss. It is truly a sculptural masterpiece. The altar, belonging to the largest pentaptychs in Europe, presents the life of St. Mary – the patron Saint of the church. The sculpted story begins with the presentation of Her family-tree and is concluded with the scene of Our Lady's coronation. This monumental work of art was created in the years 1477–1489 and it forever linked the name of its author, Veit Stoss, with Kraków.

Arcades decorate the yard of Collegium Maius, the oldest building of the Jagiellonian University in Kraków. Queen Jadwiga, devoted to the idea of renovating the of the university founded by King Casimir the Great in 1364, donated her funds, jewels and clothes for this purpose. Year 1400 marked the beginning of the University's golden years. Its graduates include Nicolaus Copernicus, Jan Kochanowski, King John III Sobieski, and many generations of men of letters and science. The University later acquired new buildings, including Collegium Novum, a neo-Gothic building designed by Feliks Księżarski.

The Wawel Castle, which Polish kings selected for their residence, was built on a limestone rock. The early settlements on Wawel Hill date back to the tenth century and the reign of King Boleslaus the Brave. Under the present-day castle, there are remnants of the Romanesque buildings – the Rotunda of St. Felix and Audauctus. The Cathedral towers overshadow the Royal Castle and the Renaissance yard, all surrounded by walls.

Tradition links Wawel Hill with the nearby monastery of the Pauline Fathers at Skałka. St. Michael's Church, which was within the monastery, over the Vistula, was the place of the execution of a Kraków Bishop, Stanisław Szczepanowski, carried out by the order of King Boleslaus the Bold.

This tragic epilogue of the conflict of the royal and ecclesiastical powers became the source of the cult of St. Stanislaus, whose figure can be seen over in a pond in front of the church at Skałka.

NON·NOBIS·DOMINE·NON

In the year 1000, a bishopric subject to the Metropolis of Gniezno was established in Kraków. The cathedral on Wawel Hill became the center of religious and state events. A Gothic church, with its three towers visible over the castle walls, was built there on the site of the early pre-Romanesque church. This was the place of numerous coronations of Polish kings and also one of their biggest necropolises. Inside the cathedral, the numerous works of art constitute the testimonies of centuries gone by. There are sculpted and canopied sarcophagi of the rulers, altarpieces, murals and woodcarvings. The focal point is the shrine of St. Stanislaus the Bishop, with the sepulcher and reliquary of the martyr.

The places of remembrance, such as the Rakowice cemetery and the former Jewish district of Kazimierz, are special sights in Kraków. Rakowice, one of the largest Polish necropolises beside Powązki in Warsaw, is a place where the memory of Polish national heroes as well as of eminent people of culture, art and literature is preserved. It also constitutes a unique collection of sepulchral art specimens created by such eminent sculptors as F. Mączyński, A. Madejski and K. Laszczka. The everyday silence and ponderous atmosphere enveloping Rakowice changes on All Souls' Day when thousands of candles illuminate the cemetery.

There is also another place in Kraków where history impressed a stigma of silence. This is the district of Kazimierz, with its old synagogues, streets deprived of their former liveliness and the cemeteries miraculously saved from the ravages and destruction of the war. The Remuh Synagogue was erected at the end of the 16th century by Israel Isserles for his son Rabbi Moses Isserles. The Rabbi became famous as a distinguished philosopher and a rector of a yeshivah. He is buried in the Remuh cemetery next to the synagogue wall. Despite the destruction brought about by the war, several hundred magnificent *matzevahs* have survived to the present time.

In the outskirts of the present City of Kraków, several dozen meters below the town of Wieliczka, an unusual underground world, exists a labyrinth of the slat-mine passageways. Salt was excavated in this area as early as the Neolithic Age. In the early Middle Ages the mine became a part of the royal estate. The rock-salt mined here was a particularly precious mineral and was considered a significant source of income for the Royal Treasury. The real labyrinth of the passage-ways, chambers and brine lakes occupies several levels underground. This is material evidence of the hundreds of years of mining in Wieliczka. Beauty is set here in extraordinary forms of salt dripstones, glittering crystals and ancient mining

tools covered with a white salt "moss." Huge specimens of mining equipment, hundreds of years old, can be seen in the part of the mine that is open to visitors. One of the exhibits is the 17th-century windlass in Moden's Chamber.

Prominent, whitish rocks among the hills overgrown with woods, shady valleys with brooks as well as rocky ravines and caves make the picturesque landscape of the Kraków–Częstochowa Jura. Numerous fortresses, called Eagle's Nests, are situated on the tops of the hills, which are natural defensive points. In the Ojców National Park, most noticeable is a 13th-century castle that was later enlarged by King Casimir the Great.

Ogrodzieniec, a small town on the border of the Częstochowa Upland, boasts the ruins of a Gothic and Renaissance castle built in the 14th century. Limestone rock, typical of this area, supports the walls and the bastions of the fortress, whose ownership changed many times throughout the centuries. In the 16th century it used to be the family nest of such families as Sulimczyk, Boner, Firlej and Warszycki. In the last years of its grandeur the castle belonged to the Męciński family.

History did not spare that magnificent edifice. The castle was burnt by the Swedes in 1655–1657 and than was seized and plundered by the Austrian army.

The Valley of Prądnik, a small rivulet, winds among the wooded hills of the Ojców National Park. In winter time, the brook and other tripping streams are covered with ice and the trees are adorned with whitish hoar-frost. The Gothic and Renaissance castle structure towers above the frozen waters. Centuries ago it was probably one of the strongholds on the trail running along the valley. The castle dates from the 14th century. Its Gothic structure changed its character owing to the modernization works carried out by its subsequent owners. Today the building is a splendid combination of early Gothic elements and Renaissance interior decorations.

Sandomierz: a town situated on seven hills around the Vistula River Valley, has been part of Polish history for ten centuries. It was the center of the province, formed already during the tribal era of Poland, which was distinctly separated from the Kraków province – the other province in the Małopolska region. During the reign of the first kings from the Piast dynasty it was one of the country's capitals (*sedes regni principales.*) During the time when the country was split amongst the sons of the deceased King Boleslaus the Wrymouth into numerous districts, Sandomierz was the capital of a duchy, and later a large Voivodeship. It always remained a center of religious life, a town with many churches and

monasteries, and from 1818 the center of a diocese. There are few places in Poland where in such a small area one can see so many objects of architecture and art, from Romanesque to the constructivism of the 1930s. Polish culture, science and spirituality would have been much poorer without the work of people related to Sandomierz. As Pope John Paul II said, "a strange power has settled in this town, the source of which comes from the Christian tradition."

Among fruitful orchards, hidden behind the lime trees, emerge the red walls of the Church of St James, the Apostle, founded by Iwo Odrowąż, a Cracovian Bishop. It is one of the oldest Polish churches made of brick (early 12th century). For over six hundred years the Dominican brothers were related to this place. Their monastery, the second after Kraków's, was created in 1226. It is not far from the Sandomierz Castle, which, in its oldest sections, dates from the rule of Casimir the Great. In the late 10th century, when the Sandomierz region was included into the state of the Wielkopolsk branch of the Piast Dynasty a town was created here. Perhaps this was the place wher the crusade led by Duke Hen

ry, son of King Boleslaus the Wrymouth and the first ruler of the Sandomierz Duchy created in 1138, started.

The nave of the Sandomierz cathedral is full of light, which falls through the high narrow windows cut in its Gothic walls. The scattered *putti* and the mysterious allegoric female figures intrigue and draw attention to the decorated altars, the work of Maciej Polejowski, an outstanding artist of the Polish Rococo. In the dark choir, the Byzantine frescos from the times of Ladislaus Jagiello tell the story of the life of Christ and the Holy Mother. She is the patron of this magnificent temple, funded by Casimir the Great, which used to be "the first Cathedral after the Kraków's" among the collegiate churches of the Kraków diocese. It has held the status of "bishop's cathedral" since 1818.

In the center of the sloping Main Square stands the Town Hall – a symbol of the town's government. It was built by Casimir the Great in the fourteenth century, yet in the Renaissance era the attic was added, and a tower in the eighteenth century. The Town Hall has been here throughout the city's history; during the town's golden era (16th–mid-18th century), when Sandomierz was like a wide gate for distributing the harvest of the land down the Vistula, and during the years of stagnation and fall. A plate in the wall of the Town Hall commemorates the residents of Sandomierz who died defending the fatherland in 1920.

On the right bank of the Vistula River, on the slope of a hill, are situated the picturesque buildings of Kazimierz Dolny. The town was probably founded by King Casimir the Great and it was granted civic rights around 1365. Kazimierz Dolny owed its dynamic development in the 16th and 17th centuries to its convenient location on the Vistula commercial trail. The town was one of the major centers of grain trade in Poland. Several granaries with characteristic ornamented façades have been preserved from that period. In the Market Square, the late-Renaissance façades of the Przybyła family's townhouses catch the eyes of the visitors. The parish church dedicated to St. John the Baptist dominates

the Market and the watch-tower soars over the panorama of the town.

Mazovia – part of Poland's historical territory during the formation of the Polish state – preserved its individual character long afterwards, an effect of the division of Poland into smaller provinces that took place at the beginning of the second decade of the 12th century. Not until the 16th century (in 1526) was Mazovia permanently incorporated into the state structure of the Polish Republic. In the same century, Warsaw, one of the Mazovian towns, began its splendid career. Warsaw was picked as the seat of the Polish throne (casting ancient Kraków into the shadows), the seat of the general parliament (Seym) of the Kingdom of Poland and the Grand Duchy of Lithuania, the place of royal elections. From that time, Mazovian territory began to become more crowded and populated. Even today, at the end of the 20th century, Mazovian landscapes are striking with their monotony – flat expanses sprinkled with the green of forests (in the vicinity of Żelazowa Wola one massive forest, Puszcza Kampinowska, has been preserved.) Of the local species of trees, the willow has won the greatest fame. It grows along the once sandy and today asphalt-covered roads of Mazovia, as well as along the banks of small rivulets, tributaries of the Vistula River. It was the Vistula, the queen of Polish rivers, which runs across the Mazovian region as well, that attracted the most settlers; on its banks, Mazovian towns, monasteries and churches appeared, like the famous abbey of Czerwińsk, not far from Żelazowa Wola, which was founded by Lateran canons regular who came to Mazovia from southern France in the middle of the 12th century. The clumps of usually old deciduous trees are another typical element of the Mazovian landscape that can be spotted from even far away.

The Mazovia Region

One such mansion was built in Żelazowa Wola, not far from Sochaczew – the ancient town of the Mazovian dukes. In 1802, Nicolas Chopin arrived at such a mansion in Żelazowa Wola. Miss Justyna Krzyżanowska, a relative to the Skarbek family, happened to live in the house. Days spent under one roof ignited the flame of mutual affection. On June 2, 1806, in the monumental Renaissance parish church in Brochów (which is one of the very few Polish churches that was built as a fortress) Nicolas wedded Justyna. Almost a year later, on April 6, 1807, first-born Ludwika came into the world; and three years later, on February 22, 1810, Fryderyk was born.

Żelazowa Wola

Warsaw

Jerzy Waldorff

Among the capitals of Central Europe ranging from Bucharest, Budapest and Prague to Copenhagen, it is the history of Warsaw that will rouse horror, compassion and, finally, admiration in a scrupulous researcher. Like an inn, difficult to defend on the crossing of international roads, Warsaw was burned, ransacked and demolished over the centuries by the armies which incessantly marched through it.

It all began with "The Deluge", when the Swedish armies ransacked the city on several times and took away anything of value. The Czarist Russia did the same, but at a slower pace, as it had more time to select what to plunder. The contents of the library of King Stanislaus Augustus, including all its furniture, was taken to Kiev. A priceless collection of tapestries that King Sigismund Augustus had bequeathed to the Polish State was stolen. Stored at the Palace of the Republic, these tapestries had been used during the coronation ceremony of Stanislaus Augustus, and now were sent north to adorn Czar residences.

The collections of the first great public library in Warsaw, founded by the Załucki family, were sent to St. Petersburg just after the third partition of Poland had taken place, as was the case with the library and with the collections of the Warsaw Society of the Friends of Sciences after 1831. The Czar's Governor, Prince Paskiewicz stole the paintings by Canaletto. When General Hurko, a notoriously famous thief, was finally leaving Warsaw, he even ordered the removal of the floor of precious wood at the Royal Palace and took the timber away. Finally, there were the Germans and the tragic year, 1944...

After each defeat, however, Warsaw had risen again, like a desperate man sentenced to death but clinging to life. After World War II, it was able to resurrect itself so that now tourists can wander again through the rooms of the Castle, and along the Łazienki and Wilanów Palaces. They would not, however, have any testimony of the existence of successive generations of the city's residents were it not for the old Powązki Cemetery.

Not only is its uniqueness notable, like every municipal cemetery, it is a continuation of life which is still vibrating in the vicinity and flowing along the streets. Though among the graves, life seems to stop for a while and all is quieter. Like Kamil Cyprian Norwid once put it "yesterday is today but moved away from us to the past." But Powązki is a remnant of the former city nearby, the city which is no more, which was murdered and turned into ruin by the Nazis. It is true that we can still live in a complex of houses, streets and squares forming the Polish capital and that this city is called Warsaw. But it is no more the pre-war, 18th and 19th-century Warsaw, of which only the iconography and the memory of a shrinking group of elderly citizens remains.

The only complete and multi-faceted record of Warsaw's everyday life has survived in Powązki – the rest was dramatically transformed. Walls were erected from the previous foundations, modern and sometimes more attractive, but devoid of the interior superposition of traditions, such as the old furniture, documents, and portraits of owners. They too have been replaced by a completely different population of newcomers, who follow different rules of behavior, live under a different political system, up to different standards, and respect new values based on new slogans.

What did the squares, houses and streets look like? What was the distinct atmosphere of the city whose pace was measured not only with rain and fine weather? This unusual capital, subjected to different restrictions under occupations, a city which was under martial law from 1862 to 1915 and could not develop normally.

If, for one reason or another, foreigners wanted to flatter the old Warsaw, they called it the Paris of the North. This would be the picture of the city that the young Artur Rubinstein had preserved for his memoirs when he was writing them in his old age. What elegant carriages were dashing through Aleje Ujazdowskie; how beautiful and elegant women were; how exquisite were the dishes served at the Bristol, not to mention the grandeur of the residences of the bankers and aristocracy!

All this is true but limited to a narrow band between Nowy Świat and Marszałkowska Streets, and from the Zamkowy Square to Belweder. Behind Senatorska Street bustled a vast Jewish ghetto, different in attire, language, religion and even scent. The poverty of Powiśle reached the escarpment of the Vistula River to Wola, a workers district, threatened with strikes just behind Marszałkowska Street; and a landed estate of a former owner of a printing house, later Baron Franciszek Szuster, extended from the Unia Lubelska Square.

When I think about the Warsaw which I had been preparing to enter as a grown-up, and later, contrary to my hopes and expectations, I witnessed the agony and death of the city, and when I reminisce of the streets, their bustling life, their different colors and different shopfront designs, where even the odors which permitted patrons to find their favorite restaurants and bistros blindfolded, when I consider all that a result of the ferment of a community over a long range of successive generations which abruptly ceased to exist, it seems to me that I am dreaming. That a city could not be here where stands the Warsaw of today, so different from that of my memories. Even though when we look at the list of streets we will still find the familiar names Podwale, Piekarska, Piwna, Rycerska, the Old Town Square.

Older citizens of Warsaw who remember their city before the cataclysm of Nazi occupation, certainly remember its abundant architectural ornaments, created mainly in wrought iron, and sometimes in cast iron. The most impressive were the stairs leading to the Town Hall, and the Opera and the Philharmonic, with railings adorned with wreaths and garlands of iron flowers and leafs. Metal lamps were lit on their platforms and here and there, one could see goddesses wrapped in cast iron chitons.

Craftsmen who practiced the art of wrought iron formed the cream of Warsaw's artisan community and set the standards for artistic crafts. In time they had either perished, or, as with what had happened after World War II, their workshops had been destroyed by the high taxes imposed on private businesses. Even when they survived the bombardments, their works deteriorated over time. The balcony railings became rusty, the sculptures were demolished, the stairs collapsed. Such works as ornamental lampposts and the wrought-iron fence surrounding Mickiewicz's Monument on Krakowskie Przedmieście are great rarities and examples of craftsmanship traditions.

Jerzy Waldorff

The Old Town in Warsaw is surrounded by a ring of the former city walls. The little townhouses, standing wall to wall with each other, line the streets demarcated centuries ago. Above their red roofs soar the towers of churches, the Royal Castle and a high column with the statue of the king who made this city in Mazovia the capital of the Republic of Poland. Not so long ago, the place was marked with insurgents' graves on which candles were burning. The "Warsaw Robinsons" coming back from their wartime wanderings made their way through the rubble. Someone who does not want to remember this should pause for a moment in front of the Archcathedral dedicated to St. John

the Baptist. There, one may read the words of Cardinal Stefan Wyszyński, engraved on the plaque commemorating the 400th anniversary of the Capital City of Warsaw. It reads: "A nation without a history and without the past becomes a homeless nation without a future."

The reconstruction of the Royal Castle, which was completely destroyed during World War II, took many years. At present it is again a prominent icon of Polish identity and its cultural symbol. Next to the castle is the Old Town, which in the summer of 1944 was an insurgents' redoubt. It was carefully rebuilt from the destruction it suffered during the war. It is now an attractive place for both the inhabitants of Warsaw and for visitors. There are numerous restaurants, cafés, galleries and souvenir shops. It gets silent and empty only in winter time after dusk.

Łazienki is a vast and exquisite park and palace complex. It consists of an English landscape park and a French-style garden with many shady alleys. Numerous antique statues hide among decorative bushes. There are also fine pavilions, including the Orangery, and some little romantic bridges over the channel. On a large pond stands the Palace on the Island and the Amphitheater modeled on the ancient amphitheater in Herculanum. Altogether this is one of the most original gardens and architectural arrangements in Europe. It was created in accordance with the orders of the last King of Poland, Stanislaus Augustus Poniatowski who was a sophisticated aesthete. He succeeded in bringing to-

the best architects and gardeners of that time and made them employ their talents for the sake of beauty. Łazienki is a symbolic place, inscribed both in the context of Polish cultural and literary tradition and in the history of the Polish national uprisings. In the 1820s, the building of the former royal kitchens housed the Military College, where the anti-Tsarist plot was initiated. On a November evening in 1830, a group of young, armed soldiers under the command of Piotr Wysocki set out from here, thus beginning the November Uprising. In the Łazienki Park is a monumental statue of the great composer Fryderyk Chopin, and in the nearby Ujazdowski Garden, Ignacy Paderewski has been commemorated.

Wilanów is a place connected with our great king, John III Sobieski. In the years 1681–1696, he had a splendid palace built. It served as the royal summer residence. The successive owners of Wilanów were the Sieniawski, Lubomirski, Potocki and Branicki families, who remodeled, extended and embellished the palace. They also increased the art collection housed in the palace and took care of the park and the double-leveled Italian-style garden with a box-tree hedgerow and geometrically-shaped lawns. The Baroque decorations of the façade depict the scenes of the King's triumphant entry to Wilanów and of his military actions against the Turks. *"Venimus, vidimus, Deus vicit"* ("We

ame, we saw and God won")
- said the King after the Vic-
ory of Vienna in 1683.

The old Warsaw cemetery is like a huge book describing two hundred years of the difficult fame and glory of the capital, so fatally situated on the European crossroads. It does not matter if these pieces of history are important with regards to public or personal matters. Walking from one grave to another is like turning over the pages of this great book, forwards or backwards, meeting unexpected events or people, standing in awe of their portraits so unlike our imagination might dictate if we knew the histories of lives of the deceased.
Two hundred years from the founding of the Powązki cemetery is enough time to accumulate the representatives of different generations and various professions. Famous or not, all of them have left their own traces on their graves, each making the picture of their times more complete, adding an indispensable element like in a puzzle game in which one piece or letter added enables us to read the whole message properly. Walking along the lanes of Powązki cemetery, one seems to be in communion with Poland, not horizontally, like in everyday life, where we meet on the common ground of the time we share, but vertically, when suddenly we come across our ancestors from the very distant – those from the 18th century under the reign of King Stanisław Augustus – to the not so distant – those who formed the independent Poland between the two world wars. Whoever enters here through the Gate of Great Silence, will find his predecessors. In the epitaphs he will read a brief story of what they were doing in life and what they contributed to their country before they had passed away.

Jerzy Waldorff

Powązki cemetery combines the beauty of the rich greenery of a park full of high trees with the natural exhibition of sepulchral architecture and sculpture. Another characteristic feature of the Warsaw cemetery is that the soil dug up to create new graves was not removed but left aside in accordance with the principles of Catholic faith, as all soil here is blessed. As a result, the ground level had gradually risen over two centuries eventually covering many graves, and offering the conservators opportunities for interesting discoveries. Conversely, despite all the cemetery has been through, hundreds of skillfully made gra… ings surrounding the tomb… richly decorated crosses, lamp… and other elements associa…

ed with the remarkable past of Warsaw's iron crafts have urvived. It is enough to point out the most beautiful to encourage visitors to look for more while wandering among the cemetery quarters. Artur Oppman, a Warsaw poet born in 1867, has left an account of a visit to Powązki with his mother in the poem entitled, "The Five Who Fell":

"I remember this day and this cemetery, and yourself,
gendarme, standing at the naked grave.
The sorrowing Christ walked along an old-fashioned lane,
as if it was a path in the fields...
(Now cross your heart my child, quickly,
here it is forbidden to pray out loud.)"

ying at the top of the Vistula River escarpment called Tumskie Hill is the oldest part of Płock, the first capital of Mazovia, a region which was once a separate duchy. After 1495, when Mazovia was incorporated into the Polish Kingdom, Płock became the capital of a voivodeship with a large population. Both the original settlement dating from the reign of Mieszko I of the Piast dynasty, and the town which received its charter in 1237, were located near the crossing of the Vistula River where important roads leading from Wielkopolska and Pomerania to Ruthenia and from the South to Prussia and Jaćwież met.

The Church of the Holy Virgin Mary of the Assumption, the Queen of Mazovia, stands as testimony to the town's long history. Belonging to one of Poland's dioceses, the cathedral was consecrated in ca. 1075, and still towers over Tumskie Hill.

In the cathedral crypt, among the tombs of other Piasts, two "rulers and heirs" of the Polish land, Ladislaus Herman (1079–1102) and his son, Boleslaus the Wrymouth (1002–1138), have found their resting place. During their reigns Płock functioned as Poland's capital.

In the western façade of the Church of Divine Wisdom in Great Novgorod, one can admire the bronze Płock Door, one of the finest works of European foundry of the twelfth century. It was made by Magdeburg craftsmen for Alexander of Malone, Bishop of Płock in the years 1129–1156, patron of the arts and founder of this Romanesque cathedral. A century later, the door was taken away by Lithuanian invaders from the north-west.

The late 16th century saw the decline of Płock's influence in Mazovia. This was due to the development of the nearby Warsaw. Standing as monuments to Płock's long history – today an important industrial centre and location of Petrochemia Co, are several old ecclesiastic and secular buildings which are still evident in the town's urban landscape, together with artefacts connected with art and culture on display at the Diocesan Museum.

After Poland's victory in the Polish-Soviet war in 1920, Płock was awarded the distinguished Order Virtuti Militari by the new Republic, in recognition of its heroic role in the fight against the Red Army.

The Cathedral in Płock, perched on a scarp over the Vistula River, was built after 1075. Originally it was a wooden church later remodeled according to the Romanesque style. The façade of the church is topped with two late-Gothic towers dating from the 15th century.

Płock

The interior of the Cathedral was illuminated for the celebration of the holy orders in 1999.
The walls are richly ornamented with neo-Romanesque murals painted in the years 1904–1914 by Władysław Drapiewski.

Toruń welcomes visitors with the towers of a medieval town hall and with the brick walls of the stronghold of the Teutonic Knights. The city was developed on the site of the former settlement, which was situated near the ford on the Vistula River, on the commercial trails leading from Hungary to Ruthenia and to Western Europe. From the first half of the 13th century the area was under the rule of the Order of Teutonic Knights. The city belonged to the Hanseatic League and in 1403 it was granted the privilege of storage. Thus it began to compete with Gdańsk and Kraków. The year 1454 in Toruń saw the outbreak of an uprising against the Teutonic Knights. After the end of the Thirteen Years' War, as a result of the Treaty of Toruń, the city was returned to Poland. Toruń impresses visitors with its beautiful medieval architecture as well as with its fine churches and streets.

APTEKA

The Gothic Town Hall in Toruń, one of the most beautiful ones in Poland, is situated in the middle of the Market Square. It was built on the shape of a quadrangle and it incorporated the buildings of the Cloth Hall, the Bread Stalls, the Town Tower and the Weigh House. Numerous modernization works carried out here brought about some architectural additions, such as the tower, the stories, the gables and the corner turrets. The charm of the Medieval, late-Gothic architecture survived in the nooks and crannies of Toruń. There are numerous tiny townhouses, granaries, as well as remnants of city walls and defensive towers.

Toruń is the birthplace of Nicolaus Copernicus (1473). His monument has a prominent place in the Market Square, in the vicinity of the Town Hall. Copernicus' House, with a painted façade, has been preserved until today.

The church dedicated to the Assumption of the Holy Virgin Mary and the former Franciscan monastery, tower over the western corner of the Market Square. Inside there are Gothic murals dating back to the late 14th century. Also the 15th-century stalls and a late-Gothic crucifix have survived.

Perched on the scarp over the Vistula River, is a Burgher's Manor House, which was built in 1489 as the seat of St. George's Brotherhood. Above it towers the Bastion Stronghold dating from the end of the 13th century. It is the oldest structure in the town.

Podmurna

In the medieval City of Toruń the most distinguished church was the Cathedral Basilica dedicated to two saints – John the Baptist and John the Evan gelist. The construction of the church began in 1270. It was subsequently re-edified in the 14th and the 15th centuries. At present its form is that of a three-aisled basilica surrounded by a ring of chapels. A monumental, 52-meter tall tower, adorned with the gilded dial of a clock, overlooks the narrow streets. The church is surrounded with luxuriant trees. On the top of the tower, its mighty 4-meter thick walls hide the famous medieval bell, the *Tuba Dei*, cast in 1500. The interior is illuminated with colorful beams of light passing through the stained-glass windows above the main altar. The late-Gothic triptych of St. Wolfgang, dating from about 1502, is situated in this prominent place.

The panorama of Toruń, as seen at sunset from the other side of the Vistula River, is the last view we gets before moving on to another city in the Vistula River Valley – the City of Malbork with the castle of the Teutonic Knights.

Malbork, a Teutonic fortress on the bank of the Nogat River, was one of the most magnificent defensive structures in Europe in the Middle Ages. Throughout the history of the independent Teutonic state, the castle was the important headquarters of the Teutonic Order. The construction of the castle began around 1278 and it was meant to be the new headquarters of the Commander of the Order, who was then abandoning its former residence in the nearby town of Zantyr. The building was erected on the peninsula surrounded with the flood waters of Żuławy (the Vistula Warpland) and the Nogat River. Its high walls were surrounded with moats, while drawbridges hindered access to the castle gates. In terms of its architectural design, the stronghold can be divided into the High Castle – with the church dedicated to the Holy Virgin Mary and the courtyard with splendid galleries – and the Middle Castle, with the Grand Master's Palace and a grand refectory.

The two-story galleries account for the beauty of the High Castle's courtyard. There is a covered well in the center of the courtyard. The overall architectural shape of the courtyard resembles that of a classic monastery viridarium. Herman von Salza, a Grand Master of the Order, was the initiator of the Order's expansion towards the East. His pondering figure guards the walls of the Malbork castle. The traditions of the medieval knighthood are nowadays continued and observed by the numerous Brotherhoods of Knights in Poland. In the castles of Malbork, Gniew and in many other medieval strongholds, they hold tournaments for knights during which they try their hand in a duel with traditional weapons.

Gdańsk

Paweł Huelle

Who were the residents of Gdańsk? Were they originally Kashubians, later Poles, and then Germans, whose civilisation, commercial relations and great entrepreneurial skills resulted in the introduction of the German language as a *de facto* official language in Gdańsk as early as the Middle Ages? It is only just to add that the population included Dutch, Scottish, British and French people, who despite their roots soon became members of the Gdańsk German-speaking elites, e.g. the Uphagen family.

Or perhaps one could state that the communities simply cohabited next to one another, with their cultures sometimes intertwining. And what about the Mennonites and Jews, for centuries kept out of the city walls? Did their identities, mainly religious, have any features specific to Gdańsk?

Similar questions may be posed when we look at the history of such cities as Vilnis and Lviv. Neither of them were originally Polish in the sense that Gniezno or Kraków were. Polish culture and language gradually prevailed, but the original Lithuanian or Ruthenian backgrounds were never completely eradicated. The issue became a matter of violent debates in the era of rising nationalism and the struggle for the creation of nation-states. Poles were satisfied with the Jagiellonian *status quo* of the past – they were free to feel at home both in Vilnius and in Lviv and would have become indignant if they were forced to speak Ukrainian or Lithuanian in these cities. There is a certain analogy with Gdańsk in this respect. From the times of Subisław, the first duke of Gdańsk and Pomerania known from written accounts, to 1918, the Polish language never disappeared from the streets of Gdańsk.

However, when the question of Gdańsk was discussed during the 1918 peace conference in Versailles, the fact that the vast majority of residents (75%–80%) identified themselves with the German-speaking area was acknowledged. Like the Lithuanians in Vilnius and the Ukrainians in Lviv, the Poles in Gdańsk were a minority. It should be openly stated that, regardless of a few exceptions, they did not belong to the higher classes of its citizens. Undoubtedly, this state of affairs was to some extent due to the years of the partitions of Poland and the Prussian Germanization policy, but it should be remembered that as early as the reign of Duke Mestwin in the late 13th century, a few years before the occupation by the Teutonic Knights, German was widely used by the owners of shops, counting houses, sawmills, ships, mills, harbors, rope making workshops, breweries, slaughterhouses and bakeries.

(...) In the 20th century, nationality has become a genetic stigma. To simply be a Gdańsk resident was not enough. One should be a German or a Pole, then a citizen of the Free City of Gdańsk. A supranational sense of belonging to a city, a little homeland, which was still possible in the 18th century, is no more that a vague memory...

The fact is that Gdańsk, a sea port, does not have a fish market. There is a market bearing this name on the Motława, but despite its historic name it has nothing to do with fish. The odor of fish cannot be discerned on the site anymore. Small fishing boats and stalls disappeared from Gdańsk cityscape for good. Those who remember the pre-war history of skippers and fishermen, smile with an air of melancholy.
One cannot say that the fish marked determined the city's identity, but when we think of Helsinki, Amsterdam or other ports where retail trade of fruits of the sea is a well-established custom, a tradition, and, last but not least, a tourist attraction, we see that a significant element of the city life has vanished. These seemingly small matters and insignificant details add up to create a broader picture. A large part of old Gdańsk was reconstructed, including the walls of townhouses and churches. Shipyards and railway junctions were put in operation, the city developed rapidly over the years following the end of the war but its function, both material and spiritual, known from the past, has been completely transformed. Thus, the question of tradition is not only how to select quotations, examples and museum exhibits but rather, like the poets say, how ready one is to listen to the walls breathing and to the rhythms of city life.

Paweł Huelle

The mighty bell-tower of St. Mary's Church, topped with a crown of spires, rises high over the roofs of Gdańsk.
St. Mary's basilica is the largest Gothic church in Poland and the largest of the brick Gothic churches in Europe. It can hold up to 25,000 people.
The three-aiseld basilica dating from 1343 was enlarged in the years 1372–1502. It was given the form of a huge hall with high windows to let in light. The main altarpiece *Mary's Coronation*, dating from 1517, is a work of Master Michael of Augsburg. The space above the chancel is closed off by a group of sculptures situated on the rood-screen beam. It is entitled *The Crucifixion* and dates back to 1517.
From 1507 till the end of WWII, St. Mary's was a protestant church. In 1992 it became a co-cathedral of the metropolis of Gdańsk.

CHRISTUS IST MEIN LEBEN
PHILIPP. I. V. 21.
JA ICH KOMME BALD
AMEN
JA KOMM HERR JESU
APOCAL XXII V 20

Numerous epitaph plaques of the burghers of Gdańsk are embedded in the floor of St. Mary's Church. The star and cell vaulting in the nave and in the aisles rests on 27 slender columns. Opposite the main entrance is the baptistery with a Baroque baptismal font dating from 1682.

The Long Market, the central place of old Gdańsk, is closed off from the east by the Green Gate – a grand palace going back to 1568. It was built by Jan Kremer who thus fulfilled the commission received from the Municipal Council. By building that edifice the burghers of Gdańsk wanted to express their gratitude to King Casimir Jagiellon for liberating them from under the domination of the Teutonic Order.

ul. Powroznicza

The former Cistercian church – the Archcathedral Basilica dedicated to the Holy Trinity – is situated in the nearby district of Gdańsk Oliwa. The most splendid showpiece inside is the Baroque organ, a masterpiece of an organ-builder – Jan Wulf of Orneta. The instrument was constructed from 1763 to 1788 and then rebuilt in 1934. At present it has almost 8 thousand pipes. The magnificent, high altar in St. John's church is made of stone. It is the only such work of art in Europe. Sculpting it took Master Abraham van dem Block thirteen years (1599–1612). The ornaments include the scenes depicting the Last Supper and the Passover, as well as the effigy of Christ in Jerusalem.

The Vistula River ends its flow in the Gulf of Gdańsk, creating a picturesque, sandy neck of land. Wisłoujście is a small fishermen's settlement belonging to Gdańsk. It was a strategic location hindering the access to the riverbed from the sea. A gothic fortress surrounded by a ring of ramparts and on the outside by a bastion-like "fort carré" was built around the light-house tower.

At the Baltic Sea

Krzysztof Burek

POLAND

The Baltic Sea – *Dominium Maris Baltici* – is a region of competition, expansion as well as co-operation of many countries and nations: Denmark, Prussia, Germany, Russia, Poland and Sweden.

Roman merchants would come to the Baltic coast for amber, also called the gold of the north. St. Adalbert, delegated by King Boleslaus the Brave, connected the Baltic seaside region to the European community of faith and culture by means of "water and spirit." Among the relics from the oldest part of the town of Gdańsk, dating from the late 10th century, archaeologists discovered a tiny wooden cross, known as St. Adalbert's cross. It must have been connected with the religious mission concluded with the death of the Patron of Poland.

"Our ancestors were content with salted, stinking fish, but we go to get the fresh one, swimming in the ocean" – these are the words of a song of Boleslaus the Wrymouth's warriors who conquered Pomerania. Written down by Gall the Anonymous, it comes back to us from the remote past.

Somewhere on the bottom of the sea, lies a ring of pure gold. In winter 1920 it was thrown into the Gulf of Gdańsk by General Józef Haller as a symbol of Poland's being wed to the sea. Two years later, the Seym of the revived Republic of Poland passed a resolution about building a harbor in Gdynia – a Polish door to the world.

The gunfire at Westerplatte, which could be heard at dawn on September 1, 1939, began World War II. Yet Gdańsk recovered from the ravages of the war. Many traditions have contributed to its present attractive and fascinating identity.

In the summer of 1980, Pomerania became the focal point of history. "Solidarity" was born here during the strikes in the shipyards on the Coast. It "opened the gates of liberty in the countries subjugated by the totalitarian regime. It pulled down the Berlin wall and contributed to the unity of Europe which after World War II was split into two camps." These are the words of Pope John Paul II, uttered on June 5, 1999, on the seashore in Sopot.

The shore of the Baltic Sea hides few reminders of the early days of the Polish state. In 1954, during the excavations made in Gdańsk, among the various fishermen's accessories, archaeologists found a tiny wooden cross. It was established that is had been a ritual token given by St. Adalbert to the baptized inhabitants of Gdańsk. At present the cross belongs to the collections of the Archaeological Museum in Gdańsk.

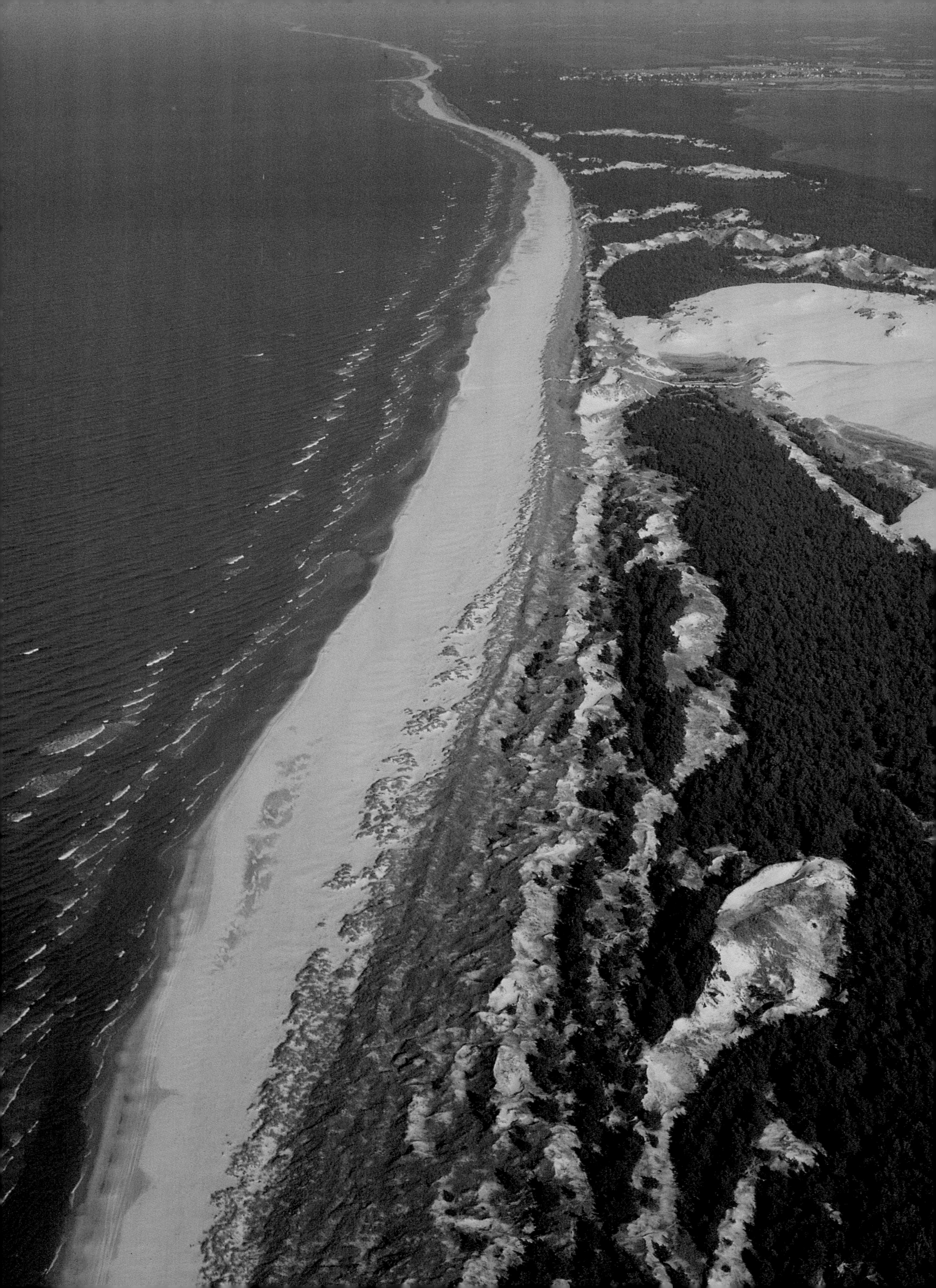

The Łeba Sandbar is a narrow stretch of a sandy land between Lake Łebsko and the open sea. It features a desert-like landscape and it is even referred to as the "Polish Sahara." The ridge of dunes, almost 20 kilometers long, occupies almost the entire width of the Łeba Sandbar. The picturesque landscapes change constantly under the influence of winds. The dunes move in a wavelike way, taking fantastic shapes and forms. In the places where the winds are particularly intensive, the dunes can move inland up to several meters a year. That is why they are called shifting dunes. The sands of the Słowiński National Park resemble a real desert so much, that the armored Africa Corps used the

area as a training-ground before their operations in Africa.

In the hours before sunset the most beautiful moments among the dunes of the Słowiński National Park occur. The last beams of light highlight the tiniest wrinkles on the sand and the regular pattern of deformations makes a fine ornament. The blades of grass on the dunes become still while the wind subsides and the sky turns purple...

The Gothic Town Hall, the Cloth Hall and the numerous Renaissance portals and façades of the townhouses are the testimonies of the former prosperity. They fill any visitor of the Market Square in Wrocław with admiration. The Market owes its atmosphere and location to Prince Henry the Bearded who established his capital city here in the 13th century. The square, measuring 175 x 212 meters, inscribed in a regular network of streets, was established then. The life of the patriciate flourished around the Town Hall. The textile trade developed in the nearby Cloth Hall, while other craftsmen – such as cobblers, saddlers or goldsmiths – had their stalls in the neighboring buildings.

Ostrów Tumski, once an island in the Odra riverbed, is the historical cradle of Wrocław. As early as the 10th century, the first residence of the Duke was established here and several years later a bishop's dwelling was built next to it. The location of the settlement was exceptionally good, since the river surrounding it made it a safe place. At the same time the nearby commercial trail contributed to its growing wealth.

At present Ostrów Tumski is a symbol of the earliest history of Wrocław. From the waters of the Odra River emerges the silhouette of the island, with two churches – the collegiate of the Holy Cross and the two-towered cathedral dedicated to St. John the Baptist.

Since in the year 1000, the
Wrocław Diocese within the
Metropolis of Gniezno was
established, there was a need
to build a church of a proper

rank. Its construction took almost two centuries and the subsequent stages of work were supervised by Bishop Nanker and Bishop Wacław of Legnica. The classic Gothic interior is covered with a ribbed vault. The main Gothic altar and the Baroque stalls are of particular beauty. The dark interior becomes illuminated during holidays and celebrations, such as the conference of the Synod of the Polish Bishops in 1999.

St. Elisabeth's chapel is a particularly beautiful part of the interior of the cathedral in Wrocław. Elisabeth, the wife of Ludwig of Thuringia, was canonized in 1215. Her relative, Cardinal Frederick Hessen von Darmstadt, who was a Bishop of Wrocław in the years 1671–1682, wanted to commemorate her. Thus, he founded a chapel richly gilded and adorned with stuccoworks. In its focal point is situated an alabaster altar with the figure of St. Elisabeth surrounded by little angels.

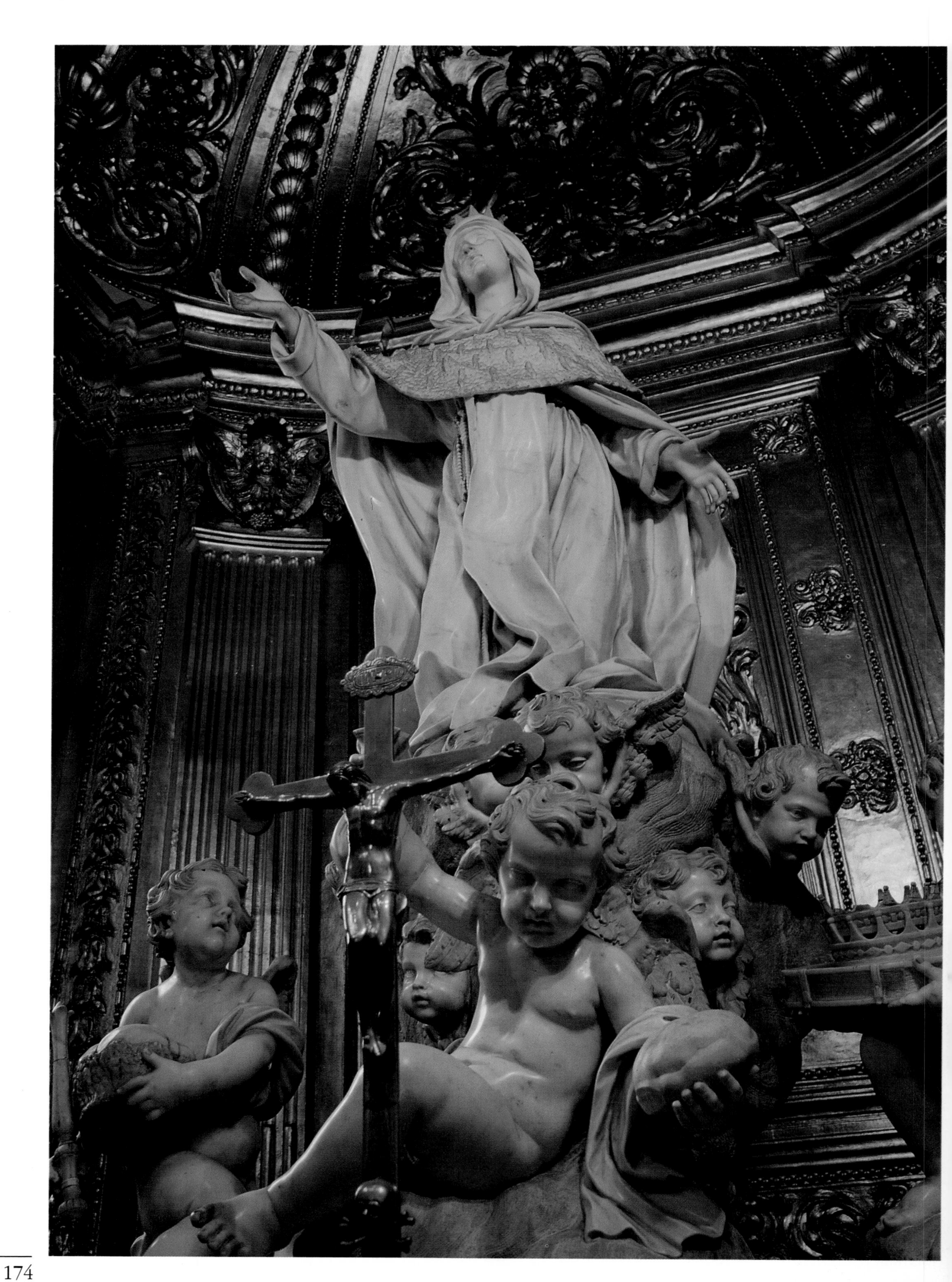

The University of Wrocław is a symbol of the long-lasting academic tradition in the city. Like in many other cities, the early educational institutions in Wrocław were connected with the Society of Jesus. A Jesuit college was founded in the city in 1639.
In 1702 Leopold I established a college called the Academy Leopoldinum. A hundred years later, in 1811 pursuant of the decision of Fredrick Wilhelm III, a merger of the Academy Leopoldinum and the Viadrina, a protestant college, took place. It gave rise to the University of Wrocław. Today it is one of the most renowned Polish universities and it has its quarters in a complex of buildings dating back to the years 1728–1742. It houses, among others, the Baroque Aula Leopoldinum, a real architectural pearl, which is ornamented with frescos, effigies of scholars and sculptures. The solemn inauguration of the academic year, which gathers the university professors, is held here every year.

The spectacular landscape of the Góry Stołowe (the Table Mountains), situated in the western part of the Kłodzko Basin, cannot be mistaken for any other place in Poland. From the ranges of the gentle wooded heights emerge high-reaching rock formations with flat tops. The upper sandstone parts of the mountains present a range of fantastic forms where numerous fissures and clefts create natural rock labyrinths.

Among the golden aura of the autumn trees, appear the rock towers of the so-called Hercules' Armory. Below, spreads a vast vista of fields and forests.

The Błędne Skały (the Erratic Boulders) constitute one of the greatest curiosities of nature in Poland. Covering an area of barely 21 hectares, the cracked sandstone rocks create a complex system of clefts and corridors and the numerous extraordinary stone formations have been arranged by Nature into a sculpture gallery. The shapes look so real that some specimens have even been given names – Rock Saddle, Mushroom, Gate. Every single glance cast at the rocks brings new associations into mind. The monstrous, several-meter tall boulders have little support. Trees and bushes have managed to creep into the narrow crevices. Tiny pools of water reflect the scanty light that reaches the bottom of the labyrinth...

The fog envelopes the woods in the Góry Stołowe National Park. The roots of the trees are set in the thin layers of soil between the rock blocks.

Podhale

Rev. Professor Józef Tischner

POLAND

Podhale is a beautiful region of proud and hardworking people, the people who are not ashamed to show who they are. The culture of the Podhale region was born in the ancient past when poverty here often meant starvation. Despite poverty this land was able to bring about the richness which is distinctly seen – it gave birth to admirable culture of its own. What is culture? It is a mirror in which the truth about human beings is reflected. It is through culture created by people that people express themselves – they talk about their misery and happiness, about their hope and despair, about walking high in the mountains and about the rest in the valleys. If you want to understand who the man is, look what he created and what he has bequeathed.

It is in the mirror of culture that we can see and understand people. We understand ourselves as well. This is the meaning and the value of culture for us. We say "every nation has its own culture". What does it mean "its own?" It means the culture through which we get to know and understand ourselves. When we listen carefully to the history of man as it can be found in highlander songs, we feel that it is also a story of ourselves, a story of our life, our happiness and unhappiness, our hope and despair, and our love.

One aspect of folk culture is worthy to be stressed in particular – it is close to life, as if it was a direct message on life. Contemporary times are the times of technology. But technology, however comfortable it may be, has killed our immediate awareness of life.

We no longer feel dew on the grass under our bare feet, we no longer wander in the mountains without any signs, neither we know how fresh spring water tastes after a busy day. Even if we conquer mountain tops and go hiking until we are exhausted, this is not our real life. We do it for leisure and entertainment, and not out of vital necessity.

So, if, despite all that, you wish to understand the life not restricted by the strict rules of civilization, return to folk culture.

Folk culture exists and is still alive in the Podhale region but it undergoes dramatic moments. From all sides it is encroached by the worst debris of civilization. New architecture replaces the traditional one. Modern music is louder than the ancient one. Gray, supra-continental outfit replaces colorful local costume. If only it was all!

The worst lies much deeper. A human being as he was before – a man who above all loved freedom and thus turned it into a creative force, who created the beauty and the truth of the mystery out of his deep love of freedom, is gradually vanishing.

But is he vanishing completely? Or perhaps it only seems to us? Perhaps he has hidden temporarily? Many times, on the right day – a Sunday, a church fair, a Holy mass celebrated in the chapel at the feet of Peak Turbacz – everything changes. Highlanders are highlanders again and one can hear their song over the mountain tops:

"Feather in the water
Shall sink, shall sink,
but music of freedom,
this shall never perish"

Then we can see the spirit of this soil. It is manifested so as everyone could see – it is still here.

The people united in the Podhalanie Association have a great contribution in showing "the spirit of the mountains." These people are a bit like ants, and a bit like crickets – they walk over this land and collect every piece of its old culture to form a compound whole. But from time to time they pick up their violins, they dress the traditional attire of their grandfathers and sing a highlander song:

"Oh, Podhale folks,
What shall you become
Your bones under beech tress
Your song over mountains..."

A minute, gilded figure of Our Lady of Ludźmierz is an object of special worship among the inhabitants of Podhale. The sculpture made of lime wood was probably carved in the 15th century in one of the local workshops. According to various chronicles, the beginning of the 18th century saw the early days of the religious cult of St. Mary in Ludźmierz. The coronation of the figure took place on August 15, 1963. Today the Sanctuary in Ludźmierz is the place of all important festive celebrations in Podhale. The traditional Harvest Festival is held here. It attracts crowds of mountaineers wearing the colorful regional costume. The place was also visited by Pope John Paul II.

Trzy Korony (Mt Three Crowns) is a characteristic peak in the Pieniny Mountains. Its altitude is 982 meters. Visible from a distance, towering over a gentle mountain range, it consists of several tops which together form a picturesque group of rocks. Trzy Korony is situated in the Pieniny National Park that was originally established in 1930.

The Tatras – the highest mountains in Poland – rise above the Czorsztyn Reservoir, a man-made lake created by building a dam on the Dunajec River. A panorama of the Tatras seen from a plane flying 2000 meters above ground evokes admiration with its diversity of rock formations – the soaring pikes, the snow-covered mountain-tops, the deep green valleys and the vast mountain pastures. The length of the Tatra range, measured along the ridge, is 80 kilometers. The highest mountain on the Polish side of the range is Mt Rysy, whose altitude is 2499 meters.

In winter time the Siwa Woda Brook (the Grey Water Brook) flowing along the Chochołowska Valley is covered with a thick layer of ice and snow.

The trees seem to lean under the heavy snowcaps. All of nature sinks into s winter sleep... Adam Asnyk, impressed by the beauty of the Tatras wrote:

Mountains gilded now by sun beams
Are in pink flames standing ablaze
And the azure serene sky gleams
Over the rocky ragged maze.

The woodland shades are now adorning
And they're bathed in a pearl-like glow
Which in the soft light of the morning
Through ravines makes its progress slow (...)

Today the Bieszczady is a mountainous border region in the south-eastern part of Poland. The gentle, wooded slopes of the mountains are crossed by countless streams and brooks. The highest ranges, with their grassy pastures, rise up to 1300 meters above sea level. In the past, the Bieszczady was considered to be the wildest area in Poland, while nowadays, it is visited by crowds of tourists and wanderers. In 1973 the Bieszczady National Park was established. It incorporates the particularly precious and picturesque mountain ranges. The natural reservations within the Park constitute a "refuge" for the rare specimens of flora and fauna. The thickest of the woodland are the habitat of the bear, the wolf,

he impressive Carpathian deer, the European bison and a number of other rare species of animals.

Hidden in the forests, smoke-generating stations of charcoal burning are a characteristic element of the Bieszczady landscape. Timber, the traditional natural resource of that region, is charred according to an original technology in large, metal retorts.

The beauty of the Bieszczady landscape is enhanced by the many streams and brooks flowing down through clefts and valleys. Murmuring softly among the stones of the riverbeds, the water pours over the rock steps, sometimes becoming calmer when deep enough... The water of these brooks speeds its way down to the Valley of the San River – the largest river in the Bieszczady. Originally, the idea of building a dam and a hydroelectric power plant on the San River was conceived in 1921. The construction work was completed in the late 60s. The water reservoir that was then created covers an area of 21 square kilometers and the length of its shoreline is over 160 kilometers. The enterprise was not only a way

of regulating the flow of the San River. The picturesque lake situated among the Bieszczady hills is a perfect place for resting and recreation.

The gorges of the Bieszczady brooks are particularly beautiful places where a sense of the wild prevails. The Valley of the Solinka rises up steeply over the riverbed of the brook. Its slopes are overgrown with old, oddly-shaped trees. The "Blue Whirlpools" ("Sine Wiry") Nature Reserve consists of a riverbed section of the Wotlin Brook making its way among the boulders and through the landslides. The water has worked its way between the slopes of the valley and it foams abundantly when falling over the numerous transverse steps.

The sunrise over Lake Solina emphasizes the riches of the landscape – the distant mountain ranges and the diversified shoreline of the lagoon.

Przemyśl is a town whose panorama seems to have been designed by an eminent painter. The layout of the buildings on the slope of the San River Valley, on the very edge of the Carpathian hills, resembles a cascade. Church towers rise high above the roofs of the houses. The towers of the former Carmelite monastery rise the highest; those of the Greek Orthodox cathedral and of the Franciscan church are situated at a lower level; the towers of St. John the Baptist's cathedral are visible in the background.
Perched on the slope of a hill, among the snow-covered trees, is the white tower of the Przemyśl castle built in 1340 on the site of an old stronghold which had existed there in the times of the Ruthenian dukes.

PRZEMYŚL

The strategic location of Przemyśl had an impact on its history. In the early years of its existence it was a place where the interests of Kiev Ruthenia and Poland frequently clashed with each other. It was also the site of Hungarian and Tartar invasions. It was in essence a border-town of cultures and nations. In 1540, thanks to King Casimir the Great, Przemyśl and Red Ruthenia were annexed by Poland. In the 19th century Przemyśl became a fortress-town – one of the largest military structures in Europe at that time. The design of the fortifications of the town was made by a Swiss engineer, Salis-Soglio, who served in the Austrian army. Forty-four forts were built in an area whose circumference

measured 45 kilometers. The construction of the fortifications continued right up until the outbreak of World War I. The Przemyśl fortress played an important role during military operations. In 1914 it kept back the Russian offensives. It was twice under siege and the second siege proved crushing for the defendants. The Przemyśl fortress surrendered at night, on March 21/22, 1915. The evidence of the bloodshed can be found in the Przemyśl cemeteries where Austrian and Russian soldiers are buried near each other; nearby there is also a Polish cemetery.

The San Valley is a land which brings together the cultures and religions of the Western Catholic Church and the Eastern Orthodox Church. Each year, on 19th January, the Orthodox Christians rejoice in the Jordan Celebration, i.e. the Lord's Baptism. The colorful liturgy starts with a morning mass, after which a procession goes down to the river. On a platform decorated with spruce branches, at a modest altar, the priests consecrate water by the triple immersion of a golden crucifix. A liberated dove symbolises the Holy Ghost – it is a commemoration of Christ's baptism. The consecrated water is then distributed among the believers, who take it home. As the water is said to possess special properties,

drinking it is seen as allegory of purification. The Jordan Celebration is a beautiful and moving ceremony, performed in the furthest areas of Eastern Poland. It may also become, like in Przemyśl, a meeting point of the Catholic and Orthodox Churches, as the mass is participated by believers and priests of both Churches.

On the hill over Przemyśl one can admire the Kazimierz Castle, constructed on the site of a former fort from the tenth century. The San River Valley and the strategic route to Russia were guarded from the hill for centuries. This was also the place where the Polish kings Boleslaus the Brave and Boleslaus the Bold stayed during their eastern campaigns. After 1340, when King Casimir the Great modernized fortification architecture throughout Poland, a stone castle was erected on the hill, from which remains only a Gothic gate. The following owners of the castle shaped it according to the Re naissance style, adding bas tions with attics.

n the vicinity of Przemyśl, ld trees of a magnificent sev- nteenth-century park hide ie white walls of the Krasic- i Castle. The castle was originally built as a quadrangle with bastions, as Stanisław Krasicki intended it as a fort. However, in 1598, Marcin Krasicki rebuilt the family estate, changing its character into a palace. Since the mid-seventeenth century the owners of this vast estate often changed, and in the twentieth century the descendants of the famous Sapiecha family were the last inhabitants of the residence.

The Palace in Łańcut is the most magnificent of the residences preserved in south-eastern Poland. It was built according to the design of Matteo Trapola, in the years 1629-41, for Stanisław Lubomirski, a Ruthenian and Cracovian Voivode. The four-winged palace with a courtyard, orangery and a library pavillion is surrounded by fortifications built in the shape of a five-armed star. Within the area of the residence, the owners created splendid garden arrangements. The alleys lead to the rose garden, the English-style garden, the Italian-style garden and the garden of perennial plants.
In 1661, a Grand Marshal and Crown Hetman, Jerzy Sebastian Lubomirski, had the palace restored for the wedding of his daughter Krystyna and Feliks Kazimierz Potocki. The descendants of the Lubomirski and Czartoryski families, who were the successive heirs of the estate, introduced numerous modifications in the outer appearance of the palace and in its interiors. The works were conducted by eminent architects and artists. At the same time numerous objects of art were collected in the palace.
In the light of a sunset, the elements of the façade of the palace acquire special sharpness. At the turn of the 19th century, the façade was remodeled according to the design by Alberto Pio and Amando Bauqué.

The influence of the multigenerational magnate families on creating our national cultural heritage should be greatly appreciated. For many decades they collected works of art, established superb libraries and hired various masters of handicraft to do the interior decorations. One of the most exquisite interiors in Łańcut was the theater hall, decorated according to the neoclassical style, following the early design by Christian Peter Aigner (dating from around 1800). The collection of books was gathered in the library erected before 1792 and remodeled by Alberto Pio and Amando Bauqué around 1900. The interior decoration according to the Elizabethan Renaissance was based on their design. The Eastern Corridor, also called the Red Corridor, is adorned with dark pine wainscot and the walls are painted red, with monograms of Alfred II Potocki.

The sculpture gallery was created around the year 1792 by converting the corridor on the first floor for that purpose. The author of this arrangement was Jean-Francois de Thomon. The illusion paintings decorating the walls and the ceiling he designed to imitate the interior of a summer-house. The stylization is based on antique motifs and the paintings are complemented with stucco-works, bas-reliefs and mosaics. The six high windows let in beams of sunlight that make the room book lighter. The ceiling of the corridor looks like an opening in a genuine summer-house through which the sky can be seen.

The coach-house built around 1902, according to the design by Amando Bauqué, on the site of a former building dating from 1833, houses over 120 coaches, sleighs and britzkas. It is the largest such collection in Poland. Some of the exhibits came from the original collection of the Lubomirski and Potocki families. Other specimens of antique, horse-drawn vehicles were obtained after World War II from private owners.

Among the trees and bushes, on the north-western bastion of the fortifications surrounding the palace stands a gloriette designed by Christian Peter Aigner and Frederick Bauman. Its seven Corinthian columns stand on a low plinth and are topped with stucco-works featuring garland motifs.

Leżajsk, one of the oldest towns in south-eastern Poland, dates back to the fourteenth century. The initial development was possible due to its beneficial situation at the bank of the San River – a watercourse leading to Gdańsk. Leżajsk's spiritual life relied on the Bernardine Monastery, which was the centre of religious life in the surrounding villages. Construction began on the fortifications of the monastery in 1608 in the place where, according to tradition, the Holy Mother and St. Joseph appeared. A small wooden church was replaced with a late-Baroque sanctuary, constructed in the years 1618–1628 from the funds of Łukasz Opaliński, the national Marshal. The monastery is im-

pressively large, and the interior shows magnificent Baroque decorations – gold-plated altars, polychromy, and beautiful, sculpted stalls from the mid-seventeenth century.

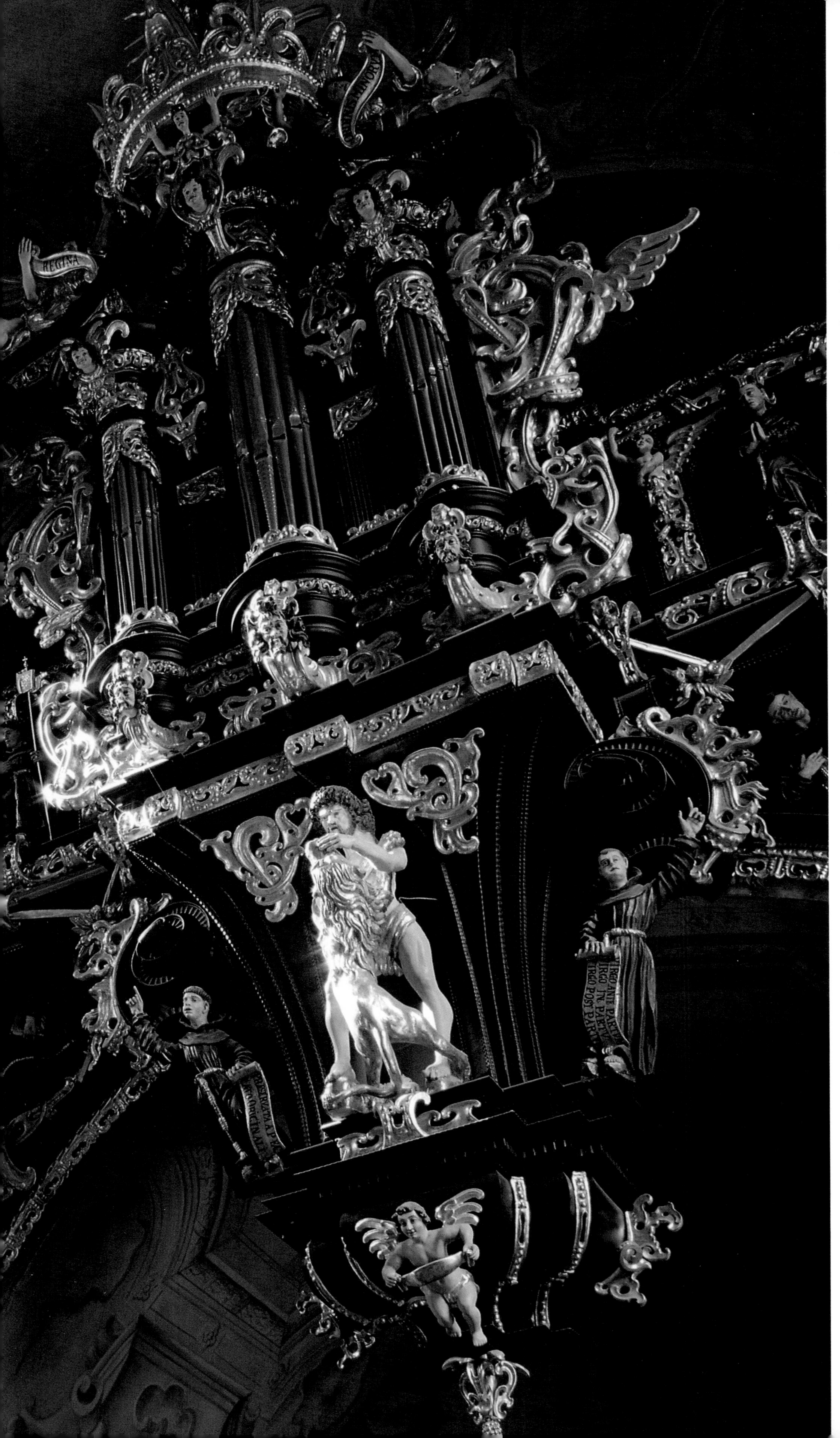

The organ in Leżajsk church, a magnificent example of Baroque art, is the largest of such instruments in Europe. It was built in two stages: the work was started by Stanisław Studziński, organ master from Przeworsk, in the years 1680–1682, and finished by Jan Głowiński from Kraków (1686–1693).

נר ה' נשמת אדם

For nearly two centuries, Leżajsk has been a living commune of two religions and communities: near the Catholic sanctuary of the Leżajsk Holy Virgin at the Bernardine Monastery, on the other side of the town, one of the main centres of the Hassidic movement in the south-eastern Poland developed. Nowadays, that the holocaust of World War II is long foregone, in March, believers from around the world gather at the tomb of a Hassid leader, Elimelech. The Hassidic movement is a special fraction of Jewish thought – its name coming from a Hebrew word *"chasid"*, meaning pious. The movement was founded by Izrael ben Eliezer, born in 1700 at the Podolia Region, where the philosophy originated.

Tzaddik Izrael ben Eliezer had many disciples, who, after his death around 1760, spread his religion across the Podolia Region, Ukraine, Belarusia, Volhynia and up to Lithuania. One of his outstanding successors was the Great Magid Dow Ber from Międzyrzecze, an expansive spiritual leader who apparently had three hundred disciples. Among them was Elimelech of Leżajsk, who popularized the Hassid thought in Poland. With his brother Meszulam Zusja of Annopol, he travelled through towns and villages as a travelling preacher, and after the death of the Great Magid in 1772, he settled in Leżajsk, where he created the centre of the Chasidic movement in Western Galicia. World War II and the trag

edy of the holocaust ended the long tradition of Chasidism in Poland. The survivors continue the dynasties of tzaddiks in Israel and the United States. Every year they come to the tomb of their tzaddik Elimelech on the anniversary of his death, to pray and leave *"kvitlech"*, little cards with requests. The tomb chapel fills with the pious crowd, prayers are heard, ritual candles are lit...

Jan Zamoyski, chancellor and hetman, a man of outstanding mind, educated at Padova, a patron of arts – this is in short a description of this statesman who, in the sixteenth century, founded the town nowadays regarded as a pearl of Renaissance art. Zamość was created as the centre of the Zamoyski estate, also called "the Zamoyski country." Intended as the capital of the region, the town, which received its charter in 1580, was built with appropriate splendour. It was designed by a Venetian architect, Bernard Morando, who surrounded the pentagonal network of streets with the rather modern fortifications In 1595 the Zamoyski Acad emy was founded. It was Ja Zamoyski, the founder, wh

had such a concept and long-term vision of the town. During his life Zamość enjoyed its boom and prosperity, it became the cultural centre of the region. After his death, Jan Zamoyski was buried in the crypt under his own chapel, which also houses ashes of his descendants. The Zamość cathedral, first a collegiate church, was built in the years 1587–1598 according to the design of Bernard Morando. It is an example of late Renaissance art, with a visible influence of Italian architecture, and is considered one of the greatest works of Renaissance art in Poland. The exterior was modified between 1824 and 1826, in order to meet the Classicist style, yet the interior remained intact.

Owing to the open mind of hetman Zamoyski, the town welcomed people from all parts of the world. The Jewish community focused around the late-Renaissance synagogue decorated with a rich attic, which has been preserved to our times. In Zamość there were also Armenian and Greek families, merchants and craftsmen. Here, the first Polish manufacture was established, which produced tapestries according to Turkish models. This ethnic diversity of the former Zamość showed in the decorations of the houses on the Main Square – in the splendid, colourful façades of the houses belonging to Armenian merchants.

The Bug River, which is of great importance in Polish history, flows majestically across a wide valley, meandering through broad meadows.

Half way through its course it cuts through the Podlasie Region, a land which has been functioning as a bridge between the Christian traditions of the East and the West, for centuries.

On the lands near the Bug River nations, cultures and religious denominations have coexisted for years, and each of them focuses around special places. The Catholics gather in Kodeń with the magnificent St. Anne's Church and the special Painting of Our Lady of Kodeń, called the Queen of the Podlasie Region. The legend has it that, the founder of the church, Mikołaj Sapiecha, stole the painting of the Madonna de Guadelupe from the Pope's chapel in the Vatican, as he was so fascinated by the image and in the state of religious obsession. Several dozen kilometres further north, the Orthodox denomination have their sacred place, Garbarka Hill, also called the Hill of Penitents. On the top, among old trees, there is a forest of crosses brought here by people, around the Kryniczka Stream which is believed to have healing powers.

The Krzna River, narrow and winding, lazily flows across the fields. The land here buries the ashes of the Tatars assimilated in Poland in the seventeenth century. The Tatar families were settled in the Podlasie region by King John III Sobieski, who in this way awarded the officers serving in the Polish army. A cemetery with several dozen stones engraved with Arabic inscriptions stands as testimony to their presence here. Further away, in Kostomłoty village, a small wooden Orthodox Church of St. Nikita is the only centre of the Byzantine-Slavic denomination. The idea of incorporation of the Orthodox Christians to the Catholic Church resulted in the creation of a “neo-union”.

A small, modest neo-union church in Kostomłoty was built in 1631, and enlarged two hundred years later. It is a simple wooden building with a small tower and hall. The interior is decorated with colourful polychromes, fittings covered with magnificent tablecloths embroidered by the parish women – the style is visibly influenced by Ukrainian art. The patron of the church, St. Nikita, was depicted in the icon by Mikołaj Baranowicz dating from the time of the church's construction. The saint is here surrounded by fourteen scenes from his life.

Kostomłoty

On the dawn of 25th June, the sun rises over the meadows on the bank of the Bug River, where a long procession passes among old oaks. These are the most important celebrations for the Orthodox Christians of this area – the Day of St. Onufry the Great, the patron of the local monastery. The legend says that once upon a time, the Bug River brought an icon of St. Onufry and tossed it on the bank of the river in Jabłeczna village, where the Saint appeared before the fishermen. On this place a chapel of the Holy Ghost was erected. Nowadays, the chapel is lit with candles, on the night of the 24th June when a mass is held on the eve of St. Onufry's Day. The day preceding the day of the monastery's

patron is dedicated to the memory of the martyr Onufry, murdered by the Bolsheviks of the Orthodox patriarch. This is a beautiful ceremony, which has a special atmosphere in this rough landscape.

Historical sources state that the monastery in Jabłeczna already existed in 1498, and the documents include a charter granted by King Sigismund the Old in 1522, which certifies that the monastery of St. Onufry was present in Jabłeczna village near the Bug River. Owners of local estates looked after the monastery, which already functioned as a parish Orthodox Church. The late sixteenth century was a difficult time for relations between the Commonwealth of Two Nations and the Orthodox Church. In 1596 in Brześć, near the Bug River, an agreement was announced, later called the "Brześć Union". Some members of the Orthodox hierarchy accepted the idea of the inclusion of the Polish Ortho

dox Church to the Catholic Church. Not all of them, however, could find their place in the new situation – and it was already a time when King Sigismund III Vasa did not approve of the Orthodox Church. The Orthodox monastery in Jabłeczna resisted the historical changes and for five hundred years persisted in performing Orthodox rites. In the entire Podlasie region, the union with the Catholic Church was not adopted by Orthodox monasteries in Brześć, Drohiczyn, and Bielsko Podlaskie. After World War II, when the Ukrainian community was forced to move to the western part of the country, St. Onufry's Monastery remained the only Orthodox Monastery in Poland.

The Biebrza National Park covers 59 thousand hectares, and it is the last such area in Europe. The Valley of the Biebrza River changes its landscape according to the seasons, and is most beautiful in spring, when the river spreads onto surrounding meadows and pastures. The wildlife, hosts the original fauna and flora – the woods here are famous for the largest population of moose, waters are full of fish, and the moors are rich with turf plants. When water rises in spring, the meadows fill with the sounds of birds – the moors are the most plentiful hatching area in Europe. Among the morning mist, one can spot the rarest species – ruffs, great snipes, as well as black and white storks and hawks.

The most beautiful season over the Biebrza River is spring. The colors of the meadows become more intensive, thousands of birds fly over the grass, the wide-reaching river meanders far into the horizon.

The river-bed near the Biebrza National Park: the meanders and old river beds are the natural habitat of the beaver. The banks are full of trees cut just above the water surface, and the branches serve the beavers to construct their lodges.

The Suwałki region is a land from a fairy tale, as many poets and writers used to say. The blue surfaces of the lakes scattered among the woody

hills, reeds rustling in the wind, and the thick pinewoods form a landscape that would appear to be created by an outstanding artist. Many years ago Aleksander Połujański described the region as follows:
"It is a beautiful land… We have treasures in earth, in water, in the woods, in beautiful landscapes, in historical monuments and in the very diversified nation itself (…). Take Switzerland and the area near the Rhone, and you shall form a landscape only similar to our area of Lake Niemen and Lake Hańcza, or the Pisna and Szeszupa Rivers, or the picturesque banks of the Augustowski Canal and the Suwałki area…"

The Suwałki Landscape Park covers an area of over 6000 ha and encompasses a group of about 20 lakes and the upper basin of the Czarna Hańcza and the Szeszupa Rivers. The picturesque landscape, which is supposed to be typical of the lowlands, surprises us with hills and valleys, numerous lakes and ponds. The horizon is dominated by Cisowa Góra Hill, also called the "Suwałki Fujijama" due to its shape. Such diversified topography is the result of the movement of the glacier in this area – thousands of years ago the lower areas of this land were filled with water from the melting glacier. This land of lakes and woods, so richly furnished by nature, was settled by man many centuries ago. The settlement

of the Jaćwingowie tribe at Castle Hill, dating from the period of the sixth to the eighth century, stands as a testimony to this fact. In more recent years, the Suwałki region was a fatherland for many nations who co-existed here. These included the Poles and Lithuanians, the descendants of the Russian Orthodox refugees of the Old Rite, the Tatars, and before World War II – the Jews and the Germans. The recent years have seen the time of closer Polish–Lithuanian relations. Attempts to find the common historical and cultural heritage have been taken by Fundacja Pogranicze (the cross-border foundation) at Sejny, housed in a restored, nineteenth-century synagogue.

On the border of the Suwałki Landscape Park and Puszcza Romincka (the Romincka Primeval Forest), in a settlement called Stańczyki, are situated the mighty historic railway bridges. They are the remains of the former Gołdap railway track running around Puszcza Romincka. The impressive construction of the Prussian engineers is based on a quite unique design concept. The concrete structure rests on a framework of huge tree trunks placed inside the monumental pillars.

STAŃCZYKI

A summer wind wrinkled the surface of Lake Holny. The access to it is hindered by green rushes and the thicket of bushes overgrowing the nearby slopes. Behind a larch-wood manor house with a large porch and a stave roof, grow old ash-trees, lindens and maples, which are the remains of the former park. In October 1989, the manor house in Krasnogruda was visited by Czesław Miłosz, the winner of the 1980 Nobel Prize for Literature, who had been away from Poland for a number of years. Once two cousins of the poet's mother, Gabriela Lipska and Janina Niementowska, lived here. In the 30's, the future author of *The Native Europe* would come here several times for vacations. His debut verse collection entitled

Three Winters (Vinius, 1933), includes two poems written in Krasnogruda. In another poem entitled *A Return* (1990), he described the impression Krasnogruda made on him when seen again after many years. It was one of these places "which my early youth once roamed through":

(...) I made my way through the thickets where the park was once but I did not find a trace of the alley.
I stood at the water and the wave surfed lightly as it did in the past,
An inconceivable identity, an inconceivable separation.

Across the woods and valleys of the Suwałki region, meandering among the fallen trees, flows the Czarna Hańcza River, known for its wild beauty and as a great canoe down flow. Lake Hańcza, the deepest lake in Poland (108.5 m), is a true wonder. This 5-kilometer long and several-hundred-meter wide lake is surrounded by steep banks covered with rocks. Trees bend over the still, dark waters, and the rough rocky banks and dark colors bear similarities to northern-European lakes.

Czarna Hańcza

A special feature to be observed in the vicinity of Lake Hańcza is the 'Bachanowo rocky area', which is a collection of several thousand erratic stones from the Ice Age. In the Suwałki landscape one can see the Church of Old Rites, a denomination of the Orthodox Church, existing in Poland since the 18th century. The history of this community dates back to 1654, when Patriarch Nikon reformed the Russian Orthodox Church, strengthening the Tsar's power. Not all priests agreed with these changes and, avoiding persecution, fled to the Suwałki region. They founded Wodziłki village, where they have cultivated their faith, language and tradition. They believe that after the death of the last priests from before the

schism, which was over two hundred years ago, they can no longer nominate their successors. Therefore, all the ceremonies are lead by the most respectable member of the local community. A few cemeteries of the Old Rite Orthodox Church have also remained hidden in the woods.

Sejny, a small town located near the border with Lithuania, is famous for its late-Renaissance Dominican monastery, the oldest part of which date from 1610. Located in its centre is the Renaissance Church of St. George, built in the years 1610–1619. The interior of the church, in the Rococo style, is furnished with 27 paintings from the turn of the eighteenth century. The Basilica at Sejny has been a pilgrimage centre due to the wooden figure of Madonna. This Gothic sculpture, dating from ca. 1400, is an interesting sacral form, called the 'cupboard Madonna', as the body of the sculpture can be opened to present the image of God the Father holding a crucifix.

The peninsula on Lake Wigry was a place of seclusion and contemplation of the Cameldolite monks. The monastery founded by King Ladislaus IV was constructed on the hill on the peninsula, which offers a magnificent panorama of the lake. The hermit huts (eremites) were erected on terraced slopes, and the monastery complex is dominated by the Church of the Immaculate Conception. After World War II the monastery buildings functioned as an arts and crafts center. The only centers of hermit life of the Cameldolite monks are the monasteries in Kraków and at Bieniszewo.

Dear Reader,

Here is my personal vision of Poland, my homeland, featuring the closer and more distant regions of my country, but all of them showing my attitude to this land.
The majority of the photographs included in this album were taken within a period of two years, 1998 and 1999. Only a small number of photographs are from my archives and a few were taken in 2000.
The selection of photographs is by no means objective. My aim was to show what is important in Polish history and what is important to me.
This album does not include a picture of the Poland of today; it is rather my impression of the presence of the Polish land in history and, especially, in European history.
More than a thousand years of Christianity in Poland have passed. Subsequent eras and generations and the recent world wars left their mark on human beings as well as on the land itself. History is still to be seen here in time-smoldered stones and images covered with patina. There are people for whom the continuation of history in their lives is of significance.
My intention was to render these reflections in photography. I took pictures of beautiful churches and necropolises, castles in which today no monarchs can be found, ceremonies of religious minorities and natural landscapes which still resist civilization.
I was assisted by co-authors, outstanding humanists who wrote about the subjects on which they are experts. Paradoxically, one of the co-authors, Jerzy Waldorff, who had been guiding us with his memories of the pre-war Warsaw throughout the recent decades, passed away during the production of this book. He wrote a few letters to me and selected the fragments of his texts to be included in this album. He passed away as if he did not want to live in the new millennium anymore. All I could do was to photograph his grave in the Powązki cemetery and include a photograph of Ignacy Paderewski's monument in Ujazdowski Park, as Waldorff requested.
Over two years a photographic picture of Poland "throughout the centuries towards the new millennium" was created. I would like to thank my Publisher and Friend, Andrzej Frukacz, for his support and encouragement that made it possible to produce this book in such a short time.
This project would not be viable without support from many other persons and institutions. I wish to express my appreciation and to thank sincerely, firstly to all of those mentioned on this page: Henryk Paner, Director, Archeological Museum in Gdańsk; Wit K. Wójtowicz, Director, Museum of the Łańcut Castle; Witold Szozda; Bernard Dąbrowski, consultant for aerial photographs; Pilots of Polish Air Club: Mariusz Szymański, Edmund Janowski, Mieczysław Pobierajło, Stanisław Jurewicz, Wojciech Polewicz; Henryk Serda, a pilot of sanitary aicraft in Kraków; Barbara and Tadeusz Owczuk, the Management of "The Place of Fryderyk Chopin's Birth" in Żelazowa Wola, but also the others friends whose names have not been mentioned.

Wydawnictwo Andrzej Frukacz
Ex Libris
Galeria Polskiej Książki

00-499 Warszawa – Poland
Plac Trzech Krzyży 16
tel. (022) 628-31-07, fax (022) 628-31-55

Publisher:
ANDRZEJ FRUKACZ

Photograps & the Concept of the Album:
PAWEŁ JAROSZEWSKI

Texts:
KRZYSZTOF BUREK, PAWEŁ HUELLE
REV. PROFESSOR JÓZEF TISCHNER, JERZY WALDORFF
PROFESSOR JACEK WOŹNIAKOWSKI

Translation:
MAŁGORZATA WALCZAK, JUSTYNA PIĄTKOWSKA, EWA BASIURA, Letterman Ltd.

Proofreading:
ALAN WALCZAK, CHRIS HOWARD, JULIE SOKOL

The texts by Jerzy Waldorff are quotations from his earlier publications
and were included upon the author's approval and his selection.
„Za bramą wielkiej ciszy" Wydawnictwo Interpress 1990

The text by the Rev. Prof. Józef Tischner was written in 1989
on the request of the author of this album.

Graphic design:
PaArt/look STUDIO

DTP:
look STUDIO
Kraków, ul. Wielopole 17
tel./fax (012) 429-18-31, e-mail look@kki.pl

ISBN 83-88455-11-7
ISBN (USA) 1-928900-04-6